THE DELAY

ALSO BY MARVIN MOORE

THE DELAY

MARVIN MOORE

Pacific Press® Publishing Association
Nampa, Idaho
Oshawa, Ontario, Canada
www.pacificpress.com

Cover design by Gerald Lee Monks
Inside design by Aaron Troia

The author assumes full responsibility for the accuracy of all facts and quotations as cited in this book.

You can obtain additional copies of this book by calling toll-free 1-800-765-6955 or by visiting http://www.adventistbookcenter.com.

All Scripture quotations in this book, unless otherwise noted, are from the THE HOLY BIBLE, NEW INTERNATIONAL VERSION®, NIV®. Copyright © 1973, 1978, 1984, 2011 by Biblica, Inc.™ Used by permission. All rights reserved worldwide.

Scriptures quoted from KJV are from the King James Version.

Scriptures quoted from NKJV are from The New King James Version, copyright © 1979, 1980, 1982, Thomas Nelson, Inc., Publishers.

Library of Congress Cataloging-in-Publication Data:
Moore, Marvin, 1937-
The delay / Marvin Moore.
    p. cm.
ISBN 13: 978-0-8163-2504-7 (pbk.)
ISBN 10: 0-8163-2504-9 (pbk.)
1. Second Advent. 2. Seventh-day Adventists—Doctrines. I. Title.
BX6154.M6236 2011
236'.9—dc23
                                                              2011028849

11 12 13 14 15 • 5 4 3 2 1

CONTENTS

Part 5: The End of the Delay

INTRODUCTION

Since about 1990, I've been giving weekend seminars in churches and at camp meetings in various parts of the United States and Canada and occasionally overseas.* One of these seminars, "Hope for the End Time," includes a Sabbath morning sermon titled "Is Jesus *Really* Coming Soon?" This book is a more comprehensive look at what is also the theme of that sermon: the delay of Jesus' return.

The pioneers of the Seventh-day Adventist Church who experienced the Great Disappointment came out of it thinking that while they'd been mistaken in believing Jesus would return in 1844, He surely would come within a few years—certainly by 1860. But Adventists had barely chosen a name for themselves by the time that year ended, and it would be another three years before they organized formally as a church. No doubt the believers who established the General Conference in 1863 were absolutely certain they would see Jesus by the year 1900—yet more than one hundred years have passed since then, and He still hasn't come! Thus, the following comment that a friend wrote to me back in the mid-1990s is understandable.

I don't mean to suggest I'm skeptical of *your* particular perspective

---

* If you would like to schedule one of my seminars for your church or camp meeting, visit my Web site at http://www.hopeseminars.org or call my office at Pacific Press: (208) 465-2577.

on the topic of last-day events. I'm skeptical of all of them. I remain open and interested in the possibility of Christ's soon return. I'm willing to suspend disbelief, but I am frankly skeptical. I do understand, in terms of our traditional story, that last-day events is our primary *reason to be,* but I wonder how long that idea can suffice as the decades rumble along—and nothing happens. Here we are 152 years beyond the Great Disappointment, still waiting. Still wondering.

Now, in 2011, when this book is being published, 167 years have passed since 1844, and we're still waiting, still wondering. How do we deal with this delay? Is there a way to explain it and still maintain our confidence in the soon coming of Jesus?

I wrote this book to respond to that apparent contradiction. I want to assure you that I firmly believe that Jesus will return soon. For much of my life, I believed that I would live to see Him come. However, I'm seventy-four years old now, and I'm beginning to suspect that, just like thousands of Adventists before me, I, too, may not live to see Jesus come. Nevertheless, like those who preceded me, I maintain my confidence that *He really is coming soon.*

In the first chapters of this book I will share with you the context of the delay, which I believe we need to know in order to understand the delay itself. Then I will explain why I believe the delay truly is almost over; I will caution you about certain misunderstandings that have arisen because of the delay; and I will discuss how we should use our time during the delay. In brief, that's what this book is about.

You're probably aware that I have written several books on end-time events: *The Refiner's Fire, The Crisis of the End Time, The Coming Great Calamity, The Antichrist and the New World Order, How to Think About the End Time, Could It* Really *Happen?* and *Challenges to the Remnant.* It's inevitable that this book will repeat some of the ideas that I discussed in those books. Where those overlaps occur, I've presented the material in summary form in this book, and I refer the reader to the books that develop the ideas in greater detail.

The underlying theme of this book is the delay. There's a tension between the belief, on the one hand, that Jesus is coming soon and the realization, on the other hand, that He hasn't returned as soon as we had hoped. My purpose in writing this book is to help you to understand that tension better and to be at peace with it.

I hope that what I have written on the pages that follow will give you the same confidence that I have: Jesus *really is* coming soon!

Marvin Moore
February 2011

PART 1

Putting the Delay in Perspective

CHAPTER 1

Abraham

Abram and Sarai were utterly discouraged. For at least forty years, they'd tried and tried and *tried* to have children, but Sarai never got pregnant. Now Abram was seventy-five and Sarai was sixty-five,* and at that age, she would no doubt have been nearing menopause.†

Today, many couples *choose* not to have children, so we might shrug our shoulders at Abram and Sarai's problem and say, "Oh well, too bad." But back then, the more sons a woman could produce, the higher the position she held in her social circles, and to not even be able to have a daughter was a social disaster.‡ Furthermore, back then, children—especially sons—were the couple's form of Social Security. Investments for retirement, monthly checks from the government, assisted living centers, and nursing homes wouldn't come on the scene for another four thousand years. A couple's children took care of them in their old age. Thus,

---

* Genesis 12:4 says Abram was seventy-five when he set out for the Promised Land, and Genesis 17:17 indicates Sarai was ten years younger.

† People lived considerably longer back then than we do today. Sarai was 127 years old when she died, and Abraham was 175 (see Genesis 23:1; 25:7). At sixty-five, she still must have had a very youthful appearance, because it wasn't long after this that Abram, recognizing her physical beauty, lied about his relationship to her because he was afraid that someone might kill him to get her (see Genesis 12:11). Thus, we can assume that she still had not reached the age of menopause, though she was no doubt approaching it.

‡ At that time, daughters were considered to be less valuable than sons.

it was with both embarrassment and trepidation that Abram and Sarai anticipated the end of her child-bearing years in the very near future.

Then one day God talked to Abram, and the news He brought was wonderful. He told Abram,

> "Go from your country, your people and your father's household
> to the land I will show you.
>
> "I will make you into a great nation,
>   and I will bless you;
> I will make your name great,
>   and you will be a blessing.
> I will bless those who bless you,
>   and whoever curses you I will curse;
> and all peoples on earth
>   will be blessed through you" (Genesis 12:1–3).

The good news was God's statement, "I will make you into a great nation." Reflect for a moment on the implication of what God said. In order for Abram to become a great nation, he would have to have at least one son. I can just see Abram rushing to Sarai at the conclusion of his conversation with God. "Sarai, guess what!" he exclaims. "We're going to have a baby!"

"Abram, please don't tease me that way."

"No, my dear, it's true! God Himself told me! He said He's going to make me into a great nation, and that can mean only one thing, my dear—you're going to have a baby boy!"

Abram can't wait till he can bounce that baby boy on his knees! But the months go by, and the years go by, and there's still no baby boy. Sarai enters menopause, and they give up hope of having a baby. But then, several years later, God comes to Abram again, and this time He is even more specific. "Look around from where you are, to the north and south, to the east and west," He said. "All the land that you see I will give to you and your offspring forever" (Genesis 13:14, 15).

Offspring! Children! Sons!

However, the years roll on as before, and still they have no children.

Then God comes to Abram a third time, and He says, "Do not be afraid, Abram. I am your shield, your very great reward" (Genesis 15:1).

I wish we knew what God intended to say to Abram next, but that information will forever remain hidden, because Abram interrupted Him. "Sovereign LORD," Abram said, "what can you give me since I remain childless?" (verse 2). In essence, Abram was saying, "God, where's this son You promised me so long ago? Sarai still hasn't gotten pregnant!"

Then Abram went on to remind God of the legal implications if he didn't have a son. He said, "The one who will inherit my estate is Eliezer." In that culture, a childless couple could adopt one of their slaves and name him as the heir to their estate. He would also care for the couple in their old age. Eliezer was Abram's most trusted servant and the logical one to fill that role.[1]

But God said, "No, Abram; this man won't be your heir. A son who comes from your own body will be your heir" (see verse 4). So now God has come right out and said it: You will have a son! The Bible says that "Abram believed the LORD, and he credited it to him as righteousness" (verse 6).*

So Abram and Sarai kept trying to have children, but Sarai still couldn't get pregnant! Now we know that men as well as women can be infertile, but they didn't know that back then. When a woman couldn't bear children, *it was always her fault.* So in her exasperation, Sarai came up with the next proposal for solving the problem. "The LORD has kept me from having children," she said. "Go, sleep with my slave [Hagar]; perhaps I can build a family through her" (Genesis 16:2). Even back then, a woman would have to have become pretty desperate before she'd send her husband off to sleep with another woman! However, in that time and place, it wasn't considered immoral for the husband in a childless

---

* This is one of the three Old Testament texts that Paul used to support his doctrine of righteousness by faith. The others are Romans 4:7, 8, quoting Psalm 32:1, 2, and Romans 1:17, quoting Habakkuk 2:4.

marriage to have a child by one of his wife's servants. This child, then, would become their legal heir.[2]

Stop for a moment and consider what rationalization Abram must have come up with. *God said the son would come from my body. He didn't say it would come from Sarai's body. OK*, Abram concluded. *I'll do it.* And nine months later, Ishmael was born. Now Abram had a baby boy to bounce on his knees!

Now think of this: The Bible informs us that Abram had a huge household consisting of more than three hundred servants (see Genesis 14:14). Given the number of children in the average family back then, it's likely that Abram was providing a living for upwards of two thousand people. That's a huge crowd for one man to support—evidence that Abram was, as the Bible says, a wealthy man* (see Genesis 13:2). And Ishmael was the heir to all of that wealth! As he grew older, everyone in the camp looked up to him as *the prince*, the child of the promise. That's what everyone believed, including Abram himself.

Thus, it was a shock to Abraham[†] when God came to him a fourth time and said, "I will bless [Sarah[‡]] and will surely give you a son by her" (Genesis 17:16). In fact, the Bible says Abraham was so stunned that he fell on his face and laughed (see verse 17). By now Sarah was eighty-nine years old.[§] No doubt she had been through menopause, and, from a human point of view, it truly was ridiculous to suppose that at her age she would bear a son. Nevertheless, a year later Isaac was born (see Genesis 21:1, 2).

Now please note this: at the ages of seventy-five and sixty-five respectively, while Abram and Sarai were still childless, God promised that He would make of Abram a great nation—which by implication meant that Abram and Sarai would have at least one son. But God didn't give them a timetable. Therefore, it's understandable that they expected this son to

---

* Abram probably acquired much of his wealth from Pharaoh, when that monarch threw Abram out of Egypt for claiming that his wife was his sister (see Genesis 12:10–20).

† God changed Abram's name to *Abraham* (see Genesis 17:4).

‡ God changed Sarai's name to *Sarah* (see Genesis 17:15).

§ Abraham said to God, "Will Sarah bear a child at the age of ninety?" (Genesis 17:17). Nine months earlier, she was probably eighty-nine.

be born fairly soon, before Sarai entered menopause, which couldn't have been far in the future. But God delayed fulfilling His promise for twenty-five years!

Abram and Sarai experienced a delay.

I find five good lessons for you and me in Abram's experience. I'll apply these lessons further in later chapters of this book, but let's look briefly at them now.

First, sometimes Abram doubted. This is evident from the fact that when God came to him the third time, Abram interrupted Him with the question, Where is this child You've been promising me? If You don't hurry up and get Sarai pregnant, there won't be a child, because she's about to enter menopause!

Similarly, Jesus hasn't returned when we've expected Him to. Because of this delay, we, too, are sometimes tempted to doubt His promise to "come again" (John 14:3, KJV).

We can also learn from Abram's experience (this is the second lesson) that despite the challenges to his faith in God's promise that a son would be born from his own body, "Abram believed the LORD" (Genesis 15:6). It takes a strong faith to believe that God will fulfill His promises when the outlook is as bleak as it was for Abram and Sarai. This is the kind of faith that God credited to Abraham as righteousness. It's the kind of faith that we need to maintain in Jesus' soon coming despite the delay.

Third, notice that God didn't credit Abram's faith in the coming Messiah as righteousness. He didn't credit Abram's faith that the lambs he sacrificed pointed forward to the Messiah. The faith that God credited to Abram as righteousness was Abram's faith that God would help him through a great personal problem. We also experience profoundly perplexing problems at times—problems that cause us to doubt whether God is on our side, and perhaps whether God even exists. It's true, of course, that God credits to us as righteousness our faith in Christ's death on the cross. But when we place our faith in God's promises in spite of our doubts, including our doubts about His soon coming, we can be sure that God also credits that faith to us as righteousness!

The fourth lesson I learn from Abram's experience is that sometimes we make mistakes because God hasn't fulfilled His promises the way we expected Him to.

And finally, while at times, Abraham showed a definite lack of faith, he eventually triumphed over his character defects. He developed such a close relationship with God that when God asked him to sacrifice his own son, Abraham obeyed! That's the kind of faith you and I need to be developing as we approach the final crisis—the one that will immediately precede Christ's return.

---

1. See the comment on Genesis 15:2 in *The Seventh-day Adventist Bible Commentary,* ed. Francis D. Nichol (Washington, DC: Review and Herald® Publishing Association, 1953), 1:311, 312.

2. See the comment on Genesis 16:2 in *The Seventh-day Adventist Bible Commentary,* 1:317.

CHAPTER 2

When the Delay Began

It seems a bit odd, doesn't it, to ask when the delay *began*? By its very nature, a delay focuses on the end point of something. What we expected to happen at a certain time failed to happen—there was a delay. But we don't have a fixed date when we can expect Christ to return. In fact, Jesus made a point of telling us that we haven't been told the time when He is scheduled to return (Matthew 24:36). It seems rather odd, then, to ask when the delay in Christ's coming *began*.

Nevertheless, I believe we can identify an approximate time when the delay began, and I'm not talking about October 22, 1844. I propose that the delay began in heaven more than six thousand years ago.

Come; take an imaginary trip with me back in time.

The Triune God was looking for someone to love. They had Each Other, of course, but that wasn't enough. So in a heavenly council that took place hundreds of thousands of years ago, or maybe even many millions of years ago, They decided to create intelligent beings who could love Them and on whom They could pour Their divine love. We know these beings as angels. The Godhead certainly must have wanted lots of beings to love, because They created millions of them! Daniel and Revelation both tell us that the angels number "thousands of thousands" and "ten thousand times ten thousand" (Daniel 7:9, 10; Revelation 5:11). Assuming that these numbers represent some degree of reality, one thousand times one thousand is a million, and ten thousand times ten thousand is one hundred million. That's a lot of angels! Not only did God love them, but they loved God, and they loved each other. There's a lot of joy in genuine love, so there must have been intense happiness in heaven. I wish I could have been there!

Now, it's the nature of love that it cannot be forced. Unless it's granted freely, it isn't love. In order to have beings whom They could love *and who would love Them in return*, the Godhead had to give them a free will. They had to give them the ability *not* to love Them if they so chose. The most exalted of the angels They created was named Lucifer, and Lucifer chose not to love One of the Members of the Godhead.

But that's getting ahead of our story.

The archangel

One of the issues that the Godhead had to deal with when They created angels was how They could present Themselves to the angels. Even if we assume that the angels were able to look at the Godhead in Their full glory, the Godhead would have been so vastly superior to and different from the angels that it would have been next to impossible for Them to fully relate to them. In order for the angels to have the closest possible relationship to the Godhead, at least One Member of the Godhead would have to step down from His high position and take on the nature of the beings They had created. So They decided that the Second Member of Their Trio would become an angel. We know Him as Michael.*

When Jesus was born on this earth, He was both fully divine—fully God—and fully human. Of course, He was fully God before His earthly incarnation too. But whether, when He took on the form of Michael, He was both fully God and fully angel in the same sense, I can't say—nor for the purpose of our discussion does it matter. The point is that the angels perceived Him as one of themselves. I especially see this in Ellen White's

---

* An addendum at the end of this chapter explains briefly why Adventists consider the biblical Michael to be Christ.

description of the origin of evil* in "Why Was Sin Permitted?" which is the first chapter of her book *Patriarchs and Prophets*.[1] I will share with you an overview.

The origin of evil

Lucifer was the most exalted of all the angels God created. I'm sure that he was also one of the most loving and lovable. And of all the angels, he held the highest position—he was the covering cherub (Ezekiel 28:14); he stood in God the Father's very presence and went on special assignments for Him. I suggest that when Lucifer was created, he was especially fond of Michael. They had different tasks, to be sure, but because Michael appeared as an angel, Lucifer thought of Him as one much like himself. Lucifer and Michael conferred frequently. They were best friends. They confided in each other. They trusted each other. *They loved each other.*

In my imagination I see Lucifer and Michael chatting with each other one day when suddenly Michael says, "I hate to interrupt, but I have a meeting to attend with the Father and the Spirit." Lucifer waves Him on with a smile, but after Michael is gone, a thought strikes Lucifer that had never occurred to him before. *Why Him and not me?* But he shrugs the question off and goes on with other business.

A few days later, however, when Michael is organizing a large assembly of angels, the question arises again. *What's so special about Him? Why can't I be the one to lead this gathering?* Along with this thought comes a feeling, an emotion Lucifer has never experienced before, one that we call jealousy. And he likes it! Then, suddenly, in what he considers to be a flash of deep insight, he thinks, *I'm as good as He is!* Upon reaching that conclusion, it seems to him that there's something downright unfair about the whole situation. This thought and the feeling that goes with it keep growing in Lucifer's mind, until being around Michael bothers him, and he starts avoiding Him.

Ellen White wrote, "Coveting the glory with which the infinite

---

* Seventh-day Adventists believe that Ellen White received the gift of prophecy and that God gave her visions and dreams about events of both the past and the future of the great controversy between Him and Satan.

Father had invested His Son, this prince of angels aspired to power that was the prerogative of Christ alone."[2] "To dispute the supremacy of the Son of God . . . [became] the purpose of this prince of angels."[3] Lucifer claimed equality with Christ.[4] I don't think he aspired to equality with *God the Father,* whom all of the angels saw in His full divine glory. Lucifer claimed equality with *Christ,* because Christ seemed to him to be merely an exalted angel like himself. He was envious as he saw Christ entering into the counsels of the Godhead while he—*the covering cherub no less*—was not invited!

I suspect that for quite some time Lucifer kept his thoughts and feelings to himself. But eventually he must have shared them with one of his most trusted friends. He probably said, "Please don't tell anyone else, but . . ." And since by its very nature, dissatisfaction has to be expressed, in due time Lucifer would have shared his feelings with another angel, and then another, and another—perhaps always with the request for confidentiality. Sooner or later, however, knowledge of Lucifer's disaffection would have spread through all the heavenly host.

The Godhead, of course, was aware of Lucifer's attitude. They knew when that first twinge of jealousy arose in his heart, and it was no doubt with apprehension that They observed his jealousy growing. Lucifer's antagonism toward Michael also "aroused a feeling of apprehension when observed by those [angels] who considered that the glory of God should be supreme. In heavenly council the angels pleaded with Lucifer. The Son of God [Michael] presented before him [Lucifer] the greatness, the goodness, and the justice of the Creator, and the sacred, unchanging nature of His law."[5] But Lucifer was unmoved.

So, in a discussion about how to respond, the Godhead decided that the Father should call a meeting of all the angels and explain to them the relationship that Michael held to the Other Members of the Godhead— that He was divine, one of Them, and thus more than merely one of the created angels. We learn of this meeting from Ellen White. She says "the King of the universe summoned the heavenly hosts before Him, that in their presence He might set forth the true position of His Son and show the relation He sustained to all created beings."[6]

Why did God have to clarify the position of His Son before the angels? I propose that it was because Michael appeared to be an angel like them, and Lucifer challenged the idea that He was anything more than that. As the Father revealed to the angels Michael's true position,

> the angels joyfully acknowledged the supremacy of Christ [that is, Michael], and prostrating themselves before Him, poured out their love and adoration. Lucifer bowed with them, but in his heart there was a strange, fierce conflict. Truth, justice, and loyalty were struggling against envy and jealousy. . . . "Why," questioned this mighty angel, "should Christ have the supremacy? Why is He honored above Lucifer?"[7]

The rebellion spreads

Now that the Father Himself had spoken, Lucifer had a choice to make: he must acknowledge the truth about Michael or persist on his own course. Unfortunately,

> leaving his place in the immediate presence of the Father, [he] went forth to diffuse the spirit of discontent among the angels. He worked with mysterious secrecy, and for a time concealed his real purpose under an appearance of reverence for God. He began to insinuate doubts concerning the laws that governed heavenly beings, intimating that though laws might be necessary for the inhabitants of the worlds, angels, being more exalted, needed no such restraint, for their own wisdom was a sufficient guide. . . . The exaltation of the Son of God as equal with the Father was represented as an injustice to Lucifer, who, it was claimed, was also entitled to reverence and honor. If this prince of angels could but attain to his true, exalted position, great good would accrue to the entire host of heaven; for it was his object to secure freedom for all. But now even the liberty which they had hitherto enjoyed was at an end; for an absolute Ruler had been appointed them, and to His authority all must pay homage. Such were the

subtle deceptions that through the wiles of Lucifer were fast obtaining in the heavenly courts.[8]

Lucifer felt flattered as one angel and then others said they agreed with him and shared his feelings. Thus, a little at a time, his discontent spread throughout heaven. Yet all along, Lucifer professed to have the best interests of the angels and the well-being of the heavenly society in mind. In everything he said, he "caused it to appear as his sole purpose to promote loyalty and to preserve harmony and peace."[9] Unfortunately, Lucifer was headed on a path toward the total destruction not only of himself but of all his angel friends as well.

The Godhead was fully aware of what was happening. Ellen White says that "such efforts as infinite love and wisdom only could devise, were made to convince him of his error."[10] And their efforts were partially successful, for Lucifer was convinced of his error, and "he nearly reached the decision to return."[11] The Godhead made it clear to him that "the time had come for a final decision; he must fully yield to the divine sovereignty or place himself in open rebellion."[12] Unfortunately, "pride forbade him" to yield to God.[13] Instead, he "fully committed himself to the great controversy against his maker."[14]

Not realizing that Lucifer had made his final decision, the loyal angels "urged him and his sympathizers to submit to God."[15] But Lucifer "denounced them as deluded slaves. The preference shown to Christ he declared an act of injustice both to himself and to the entire heavenly host, and announced that he would no longer submit to this invasion of his rights and theirs. He would never again acknowledge the supremacy of Christ."[16]

Lucifer's chief objective now was to keep as many of the angels as possible on his side. He had gone too far to turn back, but this wasn't true of the other angels.[17] However, Lucifer persuaded them that God wouldn't forgive their disloyalty. "The only course remaining for him and his followers, he said, was to assert their liberty, and gain by force the rights which had not been willingly accorded them."[18] Apparently, for the most part, the angels who had sided with Lucifer remained with him.

War in heaven

In late January and early February 2011, our television news programs featured videos of angry Egyptians pumping their fists in the air and shouting denunciations against their president, Hosni Mubarak. I picture the rebellion in heaven as being like that. In my mind, I can see Lucifer's followers, at his instigation, pumping their fists in the air and shouting, "Down with Michael! Up with Lucifer! Michael, No! Lucifer, Yes! Yea-a-a-a-a-h LUCIFER!"

Ellen White said that "God permitted Satan [Lucifer] to carry forward his work until the spirit of disaffection ripened into active revolt."[19] This is the "war in heaven" that Revelation 12:7 speaks of. War is an act of rebellion against an existing government. God has a government that rules the universe. The foundation of that government is His law of love, which has been summarized for us humans in the Ten Commandments. When Lucifer and his angels rebelled against Michael, they rebelled against God's law. "War" is a perfect description of what followed.

Apparently, God didn't intervene with supernatural power to overthrow Satan and his angels. Rather, Revelation says, "Michael and his angels fought against the dragon, and the dragon and his angels fought back." An actual battle took place that resulted in Michael and his angels throwing Satan and his angels out of heaven. On earth, armies fight it out with guns and bombs. We don't know what weapons Satan and his angels had available to them, nor do we know what weapons Michael and the loyal angels used. However, the language of Revelation suggests that the loyal angels, under Michael's leadership, had to use some form of force to eject Satan and his followers from heaven.

The delay

Now, here's a question I would like you to ponder, How long do you think it took from the moment Lucifer first became jealous of Christ until he and his angels were cast out of heaven? Ellen White says that "in great mercy, according to His divine character, God bore long with Lucifer."[20] How long did God wait to act?

Ellen White doesn't answer that question. However, if "long" had the same meaning in heaven as it's had on this earth, it could have been many years. After Adam and Eve sinned, God waited nearly fifteen hundred years for human rebellion to reach the tipping point; and after He told Noah to build the ark, He waited another 120 years before He finally loosed the Flood on the earth. I'm not suggesting that God waited that long to cast Lucifer and his followers out of heaven, but neither am I suggesting that everything happened in a year or two.

Here's another question: do you think God's loyal angels wondered when He would act?

Some time ago I heard of a couple of young adults—a brother and sister—whose parents divorced. The children had been aware of the conflict between their parents for a long time, and they knew which parent was the most to blame for the breakdown in the relationship. When the children heard about the impending divorce, they told the other parent, "We wondered how long you were going to wait to make the break." I propose that something like this must have happened in heaven. As the unrest that Lucifer was creating grew, I can imagine the loyal angels coming to Michael and saying, "Lucifer's disaffection is really becoming intolerable. When are You and the Father going to do something about it?" And Michael probably said something like, "I understand your concern, but the time hasn't come yet. Trust Me—when the time comes, the Father and I will act."

Ellen White says that

> all [of Lucifer's] acts were so clothed with mystery that it was difficult to disclose to the angels the true nature of his work. Until fully developed, it could not be made to appear the evil thing it was; his disaffection would not be seen to be rebellion. Even the loyal angels could not fully discern his character or see to what his work was leading.[21]

God waited until Lucifer and his followers broke into open revolt before He acted. In the meantime, the loyal angels had to wait. *And that's when our delay began.*

We think of the delay in terms of the second coming of Christ, but it's much more than that. The delay has to do with God's effort to settle the conflict between good and evil—what Adventists call "the great controversy." And God won't bring an end to human history until that conflict has developed on our planet to the point that the entire universe, including you and me, can see it for what it really is.

Fortunately, we can look back on six thousand years of human history and who knows how many years before that of heavenly history. For us, the delay *is* almost over. But we ask, as the angels in heaven surely must have asked during the time that Satan's disaffection was spreading, "How much longer, Lord, until this horrible situation comes to an end?" So far, God has said to us what Michael probably said to the angels: "I understand your concern, but the time hasn't come quite yet. Trust Me."

So we trust God, and we wait.

---

1. Ellen G. White, *Patriarchs and Prophets* (Mountain View, CA: Pacific Press® Publishing Association, 1958), 33–43.

2. Ibid., 35.

3. Ibid., 36.

4. Ibid., see 38.

5. Ibid., 35, 36.

6. Ibid., 36.

7. Ibid., 36, 37.

8. Ibid., 37.

9. Ibid., 38.

10. Ibid., 39.

11. Ibid.

12. Ibid.

13. Ibid.

14. Ibid., 40.

15. Ibid.

16. Ibid.

17. Ibid., 41.

18. Ibid.

19. Ibid.

20. Ibid., 39.

21. Ibid., 41.

ADDENDUM:

Is Michael Christel?

Seventh-day Adventists generally identify Michael as the Second Person of the Godhead prior to His coming to this earth as a human being. We have been criticized for this by some people because Hebrews 1:4–7 emphatically says that Jesus is not an angel. However, while not coercive, the biblical evidence supporting the view that Michael is Christ is very strong.

- Michael is called "the archangel" in Jude 9, which then says He disputes with Satan about the body of Moses. It doesn't seem likely that an angel would have the authority to do that.
- Paul, in one of his descriptions of the Second Advent, says that Christ will come "with the voice of the archangel" (1 Thessalonians 4:16).
- Daniel 12:1 introduces the end-time events, including the resurrection, with the words: "At that time Michael, the great prince who protects your people, will arise." This "great prince" is almost certainly Deity.
- The Old Testament sometimes identifies a Divine Being as "the angel of the Lord." This is especially the case in Exodus 3:2, where the "angel of the LORD" appeared to Moses at the burning bush, but when Moses asked Him His name, He said it is "I AM,"

which means "Jehovah" (literally, "Yahweh"), one of the names in the Old Testament for the Almighty God. The name "the angel of the Lord" should be understood as a title and not necessarily a description of His nature. The same would be true of Michael if He indeed is the same Person as Christ, which I believe He is.

CHAPTER 3

From Adam to Christ

He must have been one of the cutest babies that ever was born. How could it be otherwise, given who his parents were—the man and woman who came directly from the Creator's hands? I doubt there has ever been a couple more handsome or more beautiful. Human beings are an exquisite example of God's creative imagination. I enjoy the beauty of an attractive woman, and my wife says she enjoys seeing a handsome man. That's why I'm looking forward to meeting Adam and Eve in God's kingdom someday. I want to see the *original* humans, just the way God made them. Until then, I can only imagine what they might have looked like.

But that's getting off the track of my story. As I said, Cain must have been an exceptionally cute baby. And Adam and Eve had high hopes for him. Ellen White said that "when Adam and Eve first heard the promise [of a Redeemer], they looked for its speedy fulfillment. They joyfully welcomed their first-born son, hoping that he might be the Deliverer. But the fulfillment of the promise tarried. Those who first received it died without the sight."[1]

Indeed they did! The Redeemer didn't show up for another four thousand years. In our world, the delay began with Adam and Eve.

Genesis 3:15 tells us God promised Adam and Eve that the woman's Seed would bruise the serpent's head, which was a symbolic way of saying that a Redeemer would come to save fallen humanity from their sins. My guess is that God told Adam and Eve considerably more about this Redeemer than the few words we read in the third chapter of Genesis, but that's all the Bible writer recorded. Anyway, the point is that Adam and Eve looked for the "speedy fulfillment" of God's promise. They expected the Redeemer to arrive most any time. And God had promised that a Redeemer would come, *but He hadn't said when to expect Him*. It's a characteristic of God's dealings with His people through the ages that He has made promises about the first and second comings of Jesus, but He has kept His people in the dark about *when* these events would occur. He did provide, several hundred years in advance, an approximate date for the first coming of Christ (see Daniel 9:24, 25), and He has given us signs by which we can recognize when His second coming is near (see Matthew 24), but the exact times have always been a mystery.

A look at the chronology

An examination of biblical chronology suggests that the Flood occurred 1,657 years after Creation; the call of Abraham 426 years after the Flood;* the Exodus 430 years after Abraham (see Exodus 12:40); and Christ's birth 1,445 years after the Exodus. Here's how these numbers look when we add them up.

Period	Years	Total
Creation to the Flood	1,657	1,657
Flood to Abraham	426	2,083
Abraham to the Exodus	430	2,513
Exodus to Christ's birth	1,445	3,958

---

* The years for the pre- and post-Flood periods (Adam to Abraham) are based on the dates given in *The Seventh-day Adventist Bible Commentary,* 1:174–196; especially 183, 184, 191. The commentary's calculations are based on the Masoretic text of the Old Testament, which is what the majority of translators use. The Samaritan Pentateuch and Josephus give somewhat different figures for the ages of the pre- and post-Flood patriarchs.

These figures show that, from a biblical standpoint, the traditional Adventist belief that about four thousand years elapsed from Adam to Christ* is a good approximation. In the rest of this chapter I'd like to reflect a bit on the various periods into which I've divided these four thousand years.

From Creation to the Flood. Most Adventists have believed that God didn't destroy Satan and his angels when they first rebelled in heaven so He could provide a grand "show-and-tell" that would demonstrate to the angels the evil results Satan's method of governing would produce. Adventists call this show-and-tell "the great controversy." It's the theme that unites all our doctrines.

However, we can legitimately ask why God continued the experiment with sin beyond the Flood. Genesis 6:5, 6 says,

> The LORD saw how great the wickedness of the human race had become on the earth, and that every inclination of the thoughts of the human heart was only evil all the time. The LORD regretted that he had made human beings on the earth, and his heart was deeply troubled.

If by the time of the Flood, human wickedness was so widespread as to grieve God, wasn't it also bad enough to convince the angels to reject Satan's plan? Why didn't God conclude the great controversy the moment Noah and his family stepped out of the ark? I'd have stopped the experiment with sin on the spot, but I'm not God. The only answer for this question that I consider satisfactory is that the Seed of the woman hadn't been born yet. God had to allow earth history to continue long enough for Jesus to come to earth and die for our sins.

But this raises more questions. Why didn't God send Jesus to die for human sin *before* the Flood? Why wait more than twenty-three hundred years *after* the Flood to bring Him into our world?

Then think of this: we argue that in our day the delay is due to the fact

---

* Ellen White is a typical example. See *The Desire of Ages* (Mountain View, CA: Pacific Press®, 1940), 49, 117, 652, 759.

that we must warn the world of Jesus' second coming. But didn't Noah warn the whole world in his day? And if the whole world was warned then, why didn't God conclude the great controversy at that time?

Some people also argue that now God is waiting for His people to prepare themselves spiritually for Jesus' return. But it seems to me that following the Flood, the entire population of the world—*all eight people*—were on God's side. That should have been an ideal time to bring the history of sin to a close, so why didn't God do it then? I plan to ask Him that question someday—though I must also say that I'm glad He waited, because otherwise you and I wouldn't be among the redeemed!

From Noah to the Exodus. We can perhaps argue that one of the reasons why God didn't wrap up the great controversy immediately after the Flood is that He planned to establish Israel as a great nation, and He used one man, Abraham, to get that nation started. Now please remember that 426 years elapsed between the Flood and God's calling of Abraham. Why did God wait all that time before starting the nation? Why didn't He make Noah the father of many nations?

Maybe God could see that Noah wasn't the kind of person He needed to start His great nation. Perhaps He had to wait those 426 years to find the man He needed to get the job off to as good a start as possible.

Be that as it may, Abraham started the great nation with his son Isaac. That patriarch had two sons, Jacob and Esau, but only Jacob was a progenitor of Israel. Jacob had twelve sons, whose descendants became the twelve tribes of Israel. But even at the birth rates that were common back then, it took several hundred years for the descendants of those twelve men to give birth to enough people to start a nation. Did God really need to wait long enough for that to happen?

From the Exodus to Christ. At the time of the Exodus, God finally had enough people with which to start the nation He wanted to make great. At Sinai, He organized them into a governing power, but then He had another problem: they weren't exactly a shining example of loyalty to Him. He hadn't even finished giving them all the laws by which to govern their nation when they rebelled against Him by making a golden calf and worshiping it. At that point God was prepared to get rid of the whole bunch and start over again with Moses. Only Moses' intercession on the people's behalf prevented Him from doing so (see Exodus 32:1–14).

However, because of Israel's rebellion, God had to wait nearly forty more years just to get them started on the process of conquering the territory that would become their homeland. And even when they were finally settled in, they kept falling back into sin. So, God allowed foreign nations to oppress them, and then He raised up people like Gideon and Jephthah to deliver them from their oppressors. I'm sure that each time they relapsed, God hoped they would learn their lesson and follow Him more faithfully from then on, but they always fell back into rebellion again.

Of all the leaders Israel had, David was one of those who were the most loyal to God. The nation experienced its best years during David's reign and the first part of the reign of his son Solomon. Unfortunately, following Solomon's reign, the Israelites returned to their habit of rebelling against God. Among their great sins was the worship of pagan gods. It was because of this sin that God allowed the northern kingdom of Israel to be destroyed by the Assyrians, and why a century or so later, He allowed the Babylonians to conquer the southern kingdom of Judah and take most of its inhabitants captive.

The Babylonian captivity cured God's people of their idolatry, but then, in their zeal to keep the law, they lurched to the other extreme and became utterly legalistic. Part of this legalism involved a religious exclusiveness so extreme that the Jews of Christ's time considered it a sin to even shake hands with or sit down to a meal with Gentiles. Yet the Gentiles were the very people God intended them to be witnessing to! When the Jewish leaders refused to accept Jesus and in fact executed Him, God established the Christian church to fulfill His purpose of carrying the good news of salvation to the world.

Conclusions

I've raised a number of questions in this chapter for which I don't have the answers and for which I don't think any other human being on earth does either. I've asked why God apparently didn't consider the world evil enough before the Flood to persuade the angels that Satan was wrong and He was right. Why didn't He end the delay with the Flood? Why didn't He send the Seed of the woman into the world before the Flood? Why did He wait four thousand years after Adam's sin to send Christ to the world? And if His purpose was to create a nation, why didn't He start with Noah? Why did He wait 426 years to establish His nation through Abraham?

I didn't raise these questions to cause you to doubt God. I just want you to reflect on the delay. If Adam and Eve expected Cain to be the Redeemer, then every minute from their conversation with God in the Garden till Christ's first coming was a delay—which means that four-thousand-year period was one huge, long delay! I believe that delay can help us to come to terms with the delay in our day.

What we've covered in this chapter leads me to two conclusions. First, God's plans take time to develop. We've seen how long it took God to establish the Israelite nation. He told Abraham He would make of him a great nation, but He had to wait several hundred years for Abraham's descendants to become numerous enough to form that nation. Then He had to give the nation four decades to migrate to the Promised Land and several more decades to conquer it. And following this, He gave the nation nearly fifteen hundred years to accomplish its mission.

My point is that human systems develop slowly. It often takes centuries for a nation to establish itself. Cultures also change slowly, and God needed to let the angels observe the perversion of human culture as it evolved over hundreds and even thousands of years. That's the only way they could fully understand the nature of Satan's program for running the universe.

My second conclusion is also one of the most important lessons we can learn from the four-thousand-year delay between Adam and Christ: God is very patient with us and our weaknesses. Nowhere is this better illustrated than in the history of the Israelite nation. Time after time God's people rebelled; time after time He allowed them to go into captivity; and time after time He restored them and kept trying to work through them. This is an outstanding illustration of God's great mercy, of His willingness to forgive us and keep trying to use us. We can take comfort in the fact that, in spite of our failures today as Christians and as Adventists, God still wants to finish His work on earth through us.

I propose that God wasn't worried about the four-thousand-year delay leading up to the time of Christ; He isn't worried about the two-thousand-year delay since Christ's return to heaven; and He isn't worried about the delay in our day. Ellen White wrote, "God's purposes know no haste and no delay."[2] We need to apply those words to our situation.

Paul said that "when the set time had fully come, God sent his Son" (Galatians 4:4). We can be sure that when the time has fully come again, God will send Jesus back to take us home!

---

1. Ellen G. White, *The Desire of Ages*, 31.
2. Ibid., 32.

CHAPTER 4

From the Cross to the Second Coming

everal weeks after His resurrection, Jesus told His disciples, "Do not leave Jerusalem, but wait for the gift my Father promised, which you have heard me speak about. . . . In a few days you will be baptized with the Holy Spirit" (Acts 1:4, 5). The disciples obviously didn't understand the significance of what He said, because they responded with a question on a much different topic. "Lord," they said, "are you at this time going to restore the kingdom to Israel?" (verse 8). Notice that when Jesus said, "Wait for the Spirit," His disciples' immediate response was, "When are You going to establish Your kingdom?"

I think I'd have been pretty frustrated had I been Jesus. I would have wondered whether these dear disciples of mine would ever catch on to the spiritual truths I was trying to help them understand. For example, during Jesus' three and a half years of ministry, He tried numerous times to tell them about His coming crucifixion, but they always tuned Him out. (See, for example, Matthew 16:21; Luke 9:22.) And they believed Jesus was the Messiah, but their understanding of the Messiah's mission differed greatly from His—they held to the popular notion that when the Messiah came He would defeat the Romans and establish the eternal kingdom that Daniel foretold in his interpretation of Nebuchadnezzar's dream. They were expecting a triumphant Messiah. There was no room in their minds for a suffering Messiah.

The disciples were crushed when Jesus was crucified, but their grief turned to joy when they saw Him in His resurrected body. Yet forty days after His resurrection, they still held to the misconception that His mission was to defeat the Romans and establish an eternal political kingdom on this earth.

We today understand that Jesus had no intention of defeating the Romans and establishing an earthly kingdom, but please notice how similar the disciples' question is to the one we ask today. Let's modify their question just slightly: "Jesus, are You at this time going to *end the delay* in establishing Your kingdom?" Suddenly, the disciples' question sounds very familiar. Just as we do, they perceived a delay in the fulfillment of God's promises. In its details, their expectation differs from ours, but the basic issue is the same.

Jesus answered their question regarding a delay by telling them they shouldn't concern themselves about when He would establish His kingdom. He said, "It is not for you to know the times or dates the Father has set by His own authority." And instead of responding to the part of their question about what *He* planned to do, Jesus told them what He wanted *them* to do: "You will be my witnesses in Jerusalem, and in all Judea and Samaria, and to the ends of the earth" (Acts 1:7, 8). In essence, Jesus said that they shouldn't be concerned about the delay; rather, they should be concerned about fulfilling the Great Commission.

I suspect that at that moment the disciples still failed to understand what Jesus meant. A few minutes later they were staring into the heavens in awe as Jesus rose from among them and ascended into the clouds. Then two angels appeared and provided a brief answer to their question about the establishment of Jesus' kingdom. " 'Men of Galilee,' they said, 'why do you stand here looking into the sky? This same Jesus, who has been taken from you into heaven, will come back in the same way you have seen him go into heaven' " (verse 11). In other words, it hadn't been Jesus' plan to stay on earth and establish His eternal kingdom here at that time. He was on His way to heaven, and He wouldn't be setting up that kingdom until His second coming.

So the question was no longer whether Jesus would at that time establish His eternal kingdom on earth. The question was, When would He *return* to the earth to establish His kingdom? *This was a radical shift in how the disciples thought about the delay.* However, they still expected that Jesus would return right away.

The expectation of the New Testament writers

The evidence in the New Testament is quite clear that the first-century apostles expected Jesus to return in their day. Writing to the Christians in Rome, Paul said, "The hour has already come for you to wake up from your slumber, because our salvation is nearer now than when we first believed. The night is nearly over; the day is almost here" (Romans 13:11, 12). By "the day," Paul meant the day of Christ's return, and he said it was "almost here."

Lest you think Paul was alone in this conviction, please note the following statements by three of the other apostles:

- Peter: "The end of all things is near" (1 Peter 4:7).
- James: "The Lord's coming is near. . . . The Judge is standing at the door!" (James 5:8, 9).
- Jesus, as quoted by John: "I am coming soon" (Revelation 22:7, 12, 20).

You and I know, of course, that nearly two thousand years have passed since the apostles wrote these words. Why did God allow them to believe that Jesus' return was "just around the corner"?

I think there's a very reasonable answer to this question. Imagine what would have happened to the disciples' enthusiasm for preaching the gospel to the people of their generation if Jesus had told them, "Fellows, it's going to be about two thousand years before I come back. But please, till then, I want you to be very active in preaching the gospel all over the world!" The apostles would have been utterly dismayed to know that Jesus was going to wait that long to return. It would have squashed their enthusiasm flat!

But why two thousand years?

Some people suggest that Christ would have come during the New

Testament period had the early church been faithful in carrying the gospel to the world. Desmond Ford, for example, said, "The evidence of the New Testament is that Christ could have returned in the first century had the church taken the gospel to the whole world."[1]

Perhaps. Only God knows whether or not that's the case. However, allow me to share with you another possible answer. Commenting on the reason why God didn't destroy Satan at the time of Christ's death, Ellen White said that it was because "the angels did not even then understand all that was involved in the great controversy. The principles at stake were to be more fully revealed."[2] This suggests that the reason for the two-thousand-year delay is not so much the failure of the early church to carry the gospel to the world as it is the need of the heavenly beings to continue observing the outworking of Satan's rebellion.

Mrs. White didn't identify the principles the angels still needed to see worked out in real life. I'll offer three suggestions.

The evolution of Christianity. In the previous chapter, I pointed out that the earliest human culture developed over a period of about sixteen hundred years into a system that was so evil that God had to destroy it, which He did by a flood. Why didn't He send the Redeemer back once that flood had cleansed the earth? Why didn't He bring the great controversy to a close when all the wicked had been destroyed and only eight people—whom we presume all had faith in God—were left on the earth?

It seems that God realized that the angels still needed to see more evidence of evil's baleful results, so He allowed evil to develop for another twenty-five-hundred years, and then He sent His Son, the Redeemer. And why didn't God destroy evil at that point? That's precisely what the disciples asked Him—whether He was "at this time going to restore the kingdom to Israel." The answer is that God knew the angels needed to see still more of the great controversy. They needed to see the changes that took place in Christianity just as they had seen the changes in the nation of Israel, and that has taken another two thousand years.

The church was born when about 120 believers gathered in an upper room in Jerusalem in A.D. 31 (see Acts 1:15). Over the next four centuries, it spread across the Roman Empire, until by the year 400 it had become the empire's dominant—and official—religion. Four hundred years is a long time, but God had to allow that much time because church growth doesn't happen overnight. And that was only the beginning. Over the next thousand years, Christianity devolved into a semipagan religion whose adherents worshiped images, raised the virgin Mary practically to the status of a goddess, and persecuted anyone who challenged the authority of the dominant church.

God Himself foresaw all of this and even predicted it. In the seventh chapter of Daniel, He's given a snapshot of world history from Daniel's day to the end of the world. You are no doubt familiar with the symbolic presentation: A lion, a bear, a leopard, and a dragon represented the kingdoms of Babylon, Media-Persia, Greece, and Rome. That last kingdom—a major empire—was to be followed by the nations of Europe that we know today, which grew out of the barbarian incursions into the Roman Empire during the third, fourth, and fifth centuries A.D. Daniel's vision predicted that once these tribes were firmly established, a religio-political power would arise that would blaspheme God, persecute His people, and challenge His law. Blaspheming God and challenging His law is precisely what Lucifer did in heaven; and following Christ's ascension, he used the Christian religion to accomplish his purpose on earth. But Satan couldn't just snap his fingers and make it happen. He had to work patiently through the evolution of human culture and political systems.

Apparently, God saw that observing the four thousand years preceding Christ's time on earth wasn't enough to enable the angels to fully understand the terrible nature of Lucifer's rebellion. They also needed to see what would happen following Christ's crucifixion. This is my first guess as to why God gave the angels more time to observe the great controversy as it played out in human history.

A well-educated society. Consider with me what I suspect was one of Satan's major arguments in his opposition to God: "For thousands of years You've kept the human race ignorant of how nature works. People have had to live in misery because they haven't understood how to use nature to improve their standards of living. They've endured sickness without any rational way to treat their diseases. They've had to live with the most primitive technology imaginable. Let me give them the knowledge they need in order to live decent lives, and You'll see that my system of government *really can work*."*

So God said, "Go ahead, Satan. Let them develop that technology, and we'll see what happens."

It's taken a long, long time for human beings to develop that technology! The years between the fifth and the fifteenth centuries A.D. comprise the so-called Dark Ages. Whether the ignorance of humanity during this period was as great as the term *Dark Ages* suggests is a matter of debate, but there is no doubt that a revival of learning began in the 1300s that has progressed to the present time. Copernicus, an astronomer who is considered the father of modern science, lived from 1473 to 1543. The scientific revolution that his ideas sparked continued over the next five hundred years, progressing so far that human beings can now fly to the moon, perform open-heart surgery, and send e-mails from one end of the globe to another in a matter of seconds.

Has all this knowledge created a culture in which people can live in peace and harmony? Hardly! In fact, to the contrary—the increase of knowledge has made it possible for evil to be increasingly more sophisticated. Sexual perversion is pervasive on the Internet. Now human beings can blow themselves and others up by flying airplanes into tall buildings. And the world's stockpile of nuclear weapons, if set off all at once, would annihilate the human race. So much for Satan's claim that giving the human race more knowledge would demonstrate the superiority of his system of government!

Here's the crucial point: notice how much time human beings have needed to develop all this. Scientific knowledge has progressed one experiment at a time for more than five hundred years. At each stage, human beings developed new technology and built factories to make use of that technology in ways that would benefit humanity—only to tear it all down a generation or

---

* A reasonable case can also be made that God influenced the increase of knowledge and the freedom that the Western world has developed over the past several hundred years to enable His church to spread the gospel around the world in ways that would have been impossible in earlier centuries.

two later and replace it with new factories that would implement the more advanced technology that new scientific discoveries made possible.

I'm sure Jesus would have loved to come centuries and millenniums ago, but He's had to wait for the slow process of the development of human society to prove the point He wants the universe to understand.

A free society. Now let's listen to what I suspect may have been another of Satan's challenges: "God, if You will just let me develop a free, democratic society, You'll see that my system really can work."

So God said, "Go to it. Develop your free society."

Of course, Satan is the one who developed every coercive society that has ever existed. Nevertheless, out of the shambles of the horrible Inquisition, democratic governmental systems gradually evolved over several centuries, and they've given human beings more freedom than ever existed before. Unfortunately, people have perverted this liberating system, living as if it has given them a license to engage in all manner of evil and to oppose that which is good. In the name of freedom, today's secular culture is at war with Christianity and its principles for human behavior. We now hear that abortion is merely "freedom of choice," publication of the filthiest pornography is defended as a matter of "freedom of speech," and homosexual marriage is rapidly becoming a "civil right."

Ellen White didn't elaborate on the principles that the angels needed to understand better following Christ's death and resurrection. I've speculated on what some of those principles may have been. When we reach God's eternal kingdom, I'm sure we'll learn of many more. But the point I'm making for the purpose of the present discussion is that it has taken what we humans consider to be an incredibly long time for the results of these principles to become apparent. We think of this long time as a "delay" in Christ's return. God, I'm sure, thinks of it as the time it takes to ensure that when He says that final "it is finished," the great controversy will truly be *over.*

---

1. Desmond Ford, *Daniel 8:14, the Day of Atonement, and the Investigative Judgment* (Casselberry, FL: n.p., 1980), 3.

2. White, *The Desire of Ages,* 761.

CHAPTER 5

The Adventist Movement

Suppose I could have interviewed James White on October 23, 1844, and suppose that during this interview I had asked him when he expected Jesus to return. "Brother White," I would have said, "do you think Jesus will be here by 1860?"

"Oh, Brother Moore," Elder White would have responded, "Jesus will be here long before 1860!"

Or suppose that I could have interviewed John Byington, the first General Conference president, at the time the Seventh-day Adventist Church was formally organized in 1863, and suppose that during this interview I had asked him, "Brother Byington, do you think Jesus will be here by the year 1900?"

"Oh, Brother Moore," Elder Byington would have responded, "Jesus will be here long before 1900!"

That's what these pioneers believed. They were absolutely certain that Jesus would return "within the next few years"—surely within their lifetimes. They would have been utterly horrified at the thought that the year 1900 would come and go and the year 2000 would come and go and Jesus still would not have returned. Yet that is precisely what has happened, as you and I well know.

This, of course, is no different from Eve hoping that her first son would be the promised Redeemer. It's no different from the apostles in the first century believing that Jesus would surely return in their lifetimes. In the previous two chapters, I suggested some reasons why Jesus waited four thousand years after the Fall to come to earth, and why Christians have had to wait two thousand years and counting for His second coming. My basic conclusion has been that God needed to allow the angels in heaven this amount of time to observe the outworking on our planet of Satan's rebellion against Christ. The angels needed to see the great controversy develop through the evolution of human society, which is a very slow process. It took centuries for the pre-Flood society to evolve to the point that God had to destroy most of the human race and start over. It took two and a half millenniums for human society, including the nation of Israel, to "ripen" to the point where God felt it was ready for Him to send His Messiah to the world. And it has taken two more millenniums for the angels to observe the evolution of the Christian church.

So what is God waiting for now?

I'm going to venture a guess that the demonstration to the universe is probably pretty much over, and I have a biblical basis for my conclusion. It's the investigative judgment that began in 1844. If God allowed evil to continue these six millenniums to give Satan's form of government time to show its true character and thus convince the angels that God must remove it from the universe, then it seems to me that by the time God initiated a final judgment involving the angels (see Daniel 7:9, 10), the experiment had pretty much run its course. God realized that by 1844 the angels would have seen enough on which to base their conclusions about Satan's plans.

So why the 167-plus years of delay since 1844? What is God waiting for now?

A global missionary movement

Our first pioneers didn't realize that God intended them to initiate a global movement. In fact, between 1845 and about 1850, the little band of Adventists who came out of the 1844 Great Disappointment thought that most of the world was lost. They believed that in 1844 Jesus ceased

His ministry in the Holy Place of the heavenly sanctuary, shut the door to that apartment, and opened the door to the Most Holy Place, where He entered upon His Day of Atonement ministry.* They concluded this meant that Jesus had shut the door of mercy to all those who rejected William Miller's message.†

The pioneers continued to hold the "shut door" teaching for several years. But then, in November 1849, Ellen White had a vision that included a message for her husband. She told him, "You must begin to print a little paper and send it out to the people. Let it be small at first; but as the people read, they will send you means with which to print, and it will be a success from the first. *From this small beginning it was shown to me to be like streams of light that went clear round the world.*"[1] Please notice the implication of the italicized words. *Ellen White envisioned a global movement.* However, it took many more years for the Adventist pioneers, including Ellen White herself, to grasp the full meaning of her words.

By 1850, Hiram Edson had grown out of the shut-door theory to the point that he believed three classes of people could still be saved: (1) those who had not rejected the light on the Second Advent doctrine; (2) sincere people who had not heretofore made a profession of religion; and (3) children who had not yet reached the age of accountability.[2] And in that year Ellen White stressed that the "message of the third angel must go, and be proclaimed to the scattered children of the Lord"[3]—that is, to more than just the Adventist believers who came out of the 1844 Great Disappointment. In 1852, James White wrote that "if it be said that we are of the OPEN DOOR . . . we shall not object, for this is our faith."[4] So, by 1852, Sabbath keeping Adventists had pretty much turned away from their shut-door theory, but they still didn't understand that God intended them to establish a worldwide missionary movement. Then, in 1855, Joseph Bates suggested that "a few publications on the third angel's message be sent 'to some of the foreign missionary stations, especially to the

* Adventists still believe that Jesus entered upon a new phase of ministry, the heavenly Day of Atonement, in 1844. However, we also understand that He is continuing to carry out a Holy Place form of ministry, especially the forgiveness of sins and impartation of the Holy Spirit to empower believers to obey Him.

† Fittingly, ever since then this belief has been referred to as the "shut door."

Sandwich Islands [Hawaii].' "[5] That's one way the pioneers envisioned the Adventist message being carried to the whole world. Their missionary vision was further enlarged during the last half of the 1850s, as Europeans who had immigrated to America began accepting the Adventist message. By 1858, James White was encouraging the publication of the message in several of the European languages. Also, Adventists began to send out literature in response to inquiries from people still living in Europe who had heard about the Adventist message and wanted to learn more. This, these Adventists believed, was how the preaching of the gospel to "many peoples, and nations, and tongues, and kings" (Revelation 10:11) would be accomplished.[6] However, even as late as 1860, they still didn't understand that they were in the very beginning stages of an evangelistic outreach that would involve *Adventists themselves in person* carrying our unique understanding of the gospel to every corner of the globe.

The early church

This step-by-step enlargement of the church's vision is in fact very similar to what happened in the early Christian church. When the disciples asked Jesus if He was "at this time going to restore the kingdom to Israel" (Acts 1:6), He didn't answer their question. Instead, He told them about the global work He wanted them to carry out—witnessing for Him "in Jerusalem, and in all Judea and Samaria, and to the ends of the earth" (verse 8). That's similar to what God told Ellen White in her November 1849 vision—that the Adventist message would "be like streams of light that went clear round the world." However, the disciples didn't even faintly comprehend the extent of the mission Jesus' words spanned, just as our early pioneers didn't even begin to understand the implication of Ellen White's words.

At Christ's time, the Jews believed it was wrong for them to fellowship with Gentiles, including Samaritans, and the early Christian believers still held that prejudice. A year or two after Pentecost, most of them were still huddled in Jerusalem. They still had only the faintest conception of the global movement God wanted to establish through them. So God allowed persecution to break out in order to push them out of Jerusalem into Judea and Samaria (see Acts 8:1). And *surprise*—the Samaritans received the Holy Spirit! (See verses 5–17.) Then God guided Philip to an Ethiopian eunuch who was probably a Gentile convert to Judaism, and *surprise*—he accepted Jesus and was baptized! (See verses 26–40.)

A few years later, three Gentiles came looking for Peter, and the Spirit instructed him to go with them (see Acts 10:19, 20). They took him to the home of Cornelius, an officer in the Roman army who was stationed in Caesarea, where a large number of Gentiles lived. Peter acknowledged to the group gathered in Cornelius's home that social custom forbade Jews to associate with Gentiles, but he explained that he had just received a vision from God instructing him that he should "not call any man impure or unclean" (verse 28)—that's why he had come to see them. Having made that explanation, Peter preached to them, and *surprise,* once again the Holy Spirit was poured out on Gentiles!

When the leaders of the early Christian movement who lived in Jerusalem heard what Peter had done, they were horrified. They "criticized him and said, 'You went into the house of uncircumcised men and ate with them' " (Acts 11:2). Then Peter told them about the vision God had given him, about the instruction he had received from the Holy Spirit to meet with the Gentiles, and how the Spirit had been poured out on the Gentiles. And the leadership "praised God, saying, 'So then, even to Gentiles God has granted repentance that leads to life' " (verse 18). Ten or twelve years later, the Holy Spirit instructed the leaders of the church in Antioch to set Paul and Barnabas apart for a missionary venture into Gentile territory (Acts 13:2), and with this, the early church's outreach to the world began in earnest.

The point is that it took time for the early Christian church to understand the extent of the mission that God planned for it to carry out, just as it took time for the early Adventist pioneers to grasp the full extent of the mission God planned for them. Indeed, I suspect we still don't understand all that God intends to accomplish through us.

Adventist mission outreach, part 1

Adventism has had two periods of great missionary expansion.[7] The first began on September 15, 1874, with the departure of John Nevins Andrews and his two children for France.* By the year 1900, Seventh-day Adventists had established a missionary presence on every continent except Antarctica. This period of missionary expansion extended well into the twentieth century.

The names of certain missionaries were especially well known in Adventism at the time. Leo Halliwell and his wife, Jessie, used mission launches to minister to both the physical and spiritual needs of the people who lived along the Amazon River. The first mission launch, purchased in 1931 for four thousand dollars, was named the *Luzeiro,* which means "Light Bearer." It was thirty feet long and ten feet wide. The Halliwells would stock the boat with provisions, medicines, and fuel oil for the diesel engine, and then strike out on six-month trips up the Amazon River, visiting scores of villages that had no medical help other than what the Halliwells brought. Often, they would come upon villages where nearly every person was sick with malaria or smallpox. Yaws and leprosy were also common illnesses. The Halliwells injected medications and handed out pills that saved thousands of lives over the years. In the evenings, they would put up lights powered by the generator on the boat, and they would give spiritual lectures. Thousands of people gave their lives to Jesus and were baptized as a result of the Halliwells' dedicated efforts.

In Peru, Fernando and Ana Stahl ministered to the Indians around Lake Titicaca. Again, they began by meeting the health needs of the people. Elder Stahl wrote, "We found the Indians in a truly deplorable condition, living in the most abject squalor and ignorance, knowing nothing whatever of the simplest laws of hygiene, and addicted to the most horrible drunkenness and to the cocaine habit."[8] Most of the Indians never bathed or changed their clothes. The Stahls cleaned them up, treated them for their diseases, and taught them the principles of healthful living. They also shared the gospel with them, and they established churches, clinics, and some two hundred schools in the Lake Titicaca region. Today, the Colegio Adventista Fernando Stahl stands as a memorial to these valiant missionaries.

---

* Andrews's wife, Angeline, died on March 18, 1872. Their children were named Charles and Mary.

Throughout the first half of the twentieth century, stories about the Halliwells, the Stahls, and hundreds of other missionaries around the world were read as a regular part of every week's Sabbath School program. Today, many Sabbath Schools share the mission report through Power-Point programs provided by various entities in the church. And for more than a hundred years, a mission offering has been collected each week during the Sabbath School time. These funds are forwarded to the General Conference to support the church's missionary program around the world.

Adventist mission outreach, part 2

The second great period of Adventist missionary expansion began in the early 1980s. At the beginning of 1980, world membership of the church stood at just over 3.3 million[9]—a number that would have staggered the imagination of our founding fathers and mothers. Yet that was only the beginning. In 1982, the church's leadership challenged its pastors, administrators, and members to "a worldwide emphasis on evangelism,"[10] with the objective of adding one million new members to the church by the time of the General Conference Session in 1985. They called the plan "1,000 Days of Reaping."[11] During this period, membership in the church grew by 1,108,884.[12] But again, this was only the beginning. At the 1985 General Conference Session in New Orleans, Louisiana, the church's leadership introduced a plan called "Harvest 90" that challenged the church to add two million members by the time of the General Conference Session in 1990. The actual growth in membership from July 1985 to June 30, 1990, amounted to 2,303,000,[13] and by the end of 1990, membership had more than doubled to just over 6.66 million.

But again, that was only the beginning. The 1990 General Conference Session in Indianapolis, Indiana, established a department called Global Mission that in 2005 was merged with another department and renamed the Office of Adventist Mission (OAM). This department continues to the present time. The function of OAM is to identify in each division people groups among whom the Seventh-day Adventist Church has little or no representation and then develop plans to reach these groups with the Adventist message. Of special interest is the 10/40 Window, the "regions of the eastern hemisphere located between 10 and 40 degrees north of the equator" that have "the highest level of socioeconomic challenges and least access to the Christian message and Christian resources on the planet."[14] Approximately two-thirds of the global population lives in this part of the world. The people in the 10/40 Window are mostly Muslim, Hindu, Buddhist, and animist.

OAM's basic strategy has been to enlist volunteers* who are indigenous to the regions being targeted and who will agree to settle there so they can reach out to the people in that area with health and gospel evangelism. In the years since 1990, OAM has established work among relatively untouched people groups in more than two hundred countries, especially in the 10/40 Window.

In the early 1960s, Seventh-day Adventists began encouraging college students to take a year out of their studies to work as student missionaries, usually in one of the underdeveloped countries of the world. In the years since, thousands of college-age young people have devoted a year or more of their lives to mission work. They have worked in a wide variety of capacities, such as teaching at English language schools, working as assistant dormitory deans, and helping with construction projects.

Also, since about 1990, thousands of Adventists from high school age to senior citizens have spent one or two weeks to several months as short-term missionaries in underdeveloped parts of the world. These people typically raise the funds to cover all of their travel and living expenses, and, in many cases, they also raised funds for the projects they're working on. At the time this book was published, my wife, Lois, and I had traveled to India together five times to conduct evangelistic meetings, and Lois has gone to India three additional times by herself to assist with both gospel evangelism and health evangelism projects.

Adventist independent ministries

Several Adventist independent ministries have been established in recent years with the express purpose of carrying the gospel to the underdeveloped parts of the world. *The Quiet Hour* (TQH) was started as a

---

* These volunteers receive a small monthly stipend.

North American radio program by Pastor J. L. Tucker in 1937. Today, it has expanded into a global evangelistic effort that provides planes, boats, and bicycles for mission work in many underdeveloped countries. Quiet Hour Ministries (QHM) has built thousands of chapels around the world, and, in many cases, they have conducted evangelistic meetings to fill them. In February and March 2011, my wife Lois and I conducted an evangelistic series for ten villages in India, and TQH paid five thousand dollars each to build churches in these villages—a total of fifty thousand dollars. Pastor Bill Tucker, the son of J. L. Tucker, is the current director and speaker of TQH. Over the years, he and his team have conducted many evangelistic meetings in third-world countries.

Adventist Frontier Missions (AFM) is a "lay ministry dedicated to establishing church-planting movements among people groups with no Adventist presence."[15] Individuals and families from the developed countries of the world commit to stay in a particular locale for a minimum of five years, and many stay much longer. Their task is to learn the language and culture of the people they serve, become acquainted with them, share the gospel with them, and where possible, raise up churches. AFM volunteers raise the money to cover their living expenses during their term of mission service. A project is considered completed when the AFM missionaries have established a "mother church" and at least one "daughter church."

An estimated eight million people live in regions where aviation is the only means of contact with the outside world. These people are the special target of Adventist World Aviation (AWA) missionaries. AWA "exists to provide aviation and communications support to those serving the physical, mental, and spiritual needs of the unreached and forgotten peoples of the earth."[16] They establish a base facility at a hub, usually in or near a major city, with at least one small aircraft, a hangar, and pilots and mechanics to operate and maintain the planes. Then they build primitive landing strips in remote locations and send Adventist families to live there, providing them with radios to contact their regional headquarters. AWA pilots make regular trips to these airstrips, bringing supplies to both the families and the people in these areas. Often, AWA provides air ambulance service, ferrying critically ill or injured persons to medical facilities in the hub city. Many lives have been saved as a result of AWA's assistance.

Gospel Outreach (GO) "is dedicated to extending the international ministry of the Seventh-day Adventist Church in the 10/40 Window. It raises funds for local evangelists in some of the world's poorest countries."[17] GO raises funds to hire local workers who can do evangelism for a fraction of what it would cost to send someone from one of the developed countries of the world. These workers are recruited, hired, trained, and supervised by the local Adventist mission. In 2010, GO was funding two thousand local evangelists. GO also arranges projects that can be carried out by short-term missionaries from developed countries. These missionaries must cover their own expenses to do gospel and health evangelism especially in the 10/40 Window.

Maranatha Volunteers International (Maranatha) was established in 1969 for the purpose of building churches, schools, clinics, orphanages, and even hospitals in underdeveloped countries of the world. Maranatha volunteers also assist with church building projects in North America. Maranatha often arranges for volunteers to build multiple churches in a particular country or region. Once Maranatha accepts a request, they provide both construction supplies and volunteers for the project. Maranatha also coordinates fund-raising efforts for international building projects, but not for building projects in North America. Every year an average of three thousand people sign up to participate in a Maranatha project. This means that since the organization's inception, there have been more than sixty thousand Maranatha volunteers.[18]

Several other excellent independent ministries serve the Seventh-day Adventist Church in underdeveloped parts of the world. In addition, there are others that focus on serving North America. Two of the best known are the Three Angels Broadcasting Network and Amazing Facts. Each of these independent ministries is loyal to and works very closely with the Seventh-day Adventist Church and its leadership.

Conclusion

In 1900, during the church's first major mission outreach, global membership stood at a little over seven thousand, most of it in North America. The church passed the one-million mark in 1955, the two-million mark in 1970, and the three-million mark in 1978. Early in the 1980s, the church embarked on its second major mission outreach with the "1,000 Days of Reaping," "Harvest 90," and Global Mission (now Office of Adventist Mission), which I've described in this chapter. As a result of these efforts and those of several major independent ministries, the church's accessions (new members joining the church) exceeded one million in 2004, and it has maintained that rate of growth every year since. At the time of the 2010 General Conference Session in Atlanta, Georgia, world membership stood at just under sixteen million, and by the time you read these words it will almost certainly have reached seventeen million, and very likely much more.

The pioneers of the Seventh-day Adventist Church who came out of the Great Disappointment in 1844 hadn't the slightest conception of what their movement would become, nor is it likely they would have believed it, had someone told them. However, Ellen White's vision back in 1849 of a missionary movement that would spread "like streams of light that went clear round the world" has been fulfilled in a most remarkable way. Yet I propose that we in the second decade of the twenty-first century still have a very limited understanding of God's plans for this movement.

For more than 150 years, Seventh-day Adventists have believed and preached that Jesus is coming soon. Every generation of Adventists has been certain that Jesus would return in its day. Yet here we are, more than 160 years beyond the Great Disappointment, and He still hasn't come. Why? Why have so many Adventists who expected Jesus to return during their lifetimes gone to their graves with disappointed hopes? Was something wrong with their faith? Is Jesus really *not* coming soon?

From what I've shared with you in this chapter, I trust you can see that it would have been impossible for God to develop within a few years of the Great Disappointment the global movement we have become. Establishing educational and medical institutions around the world requires a lot of time. Bringing the church's membership to what it is today has taken years and years of patient labor by thousands—and today, millions—of people all over the world who win other people to Jesus one at a time.

I propose that one major reason for what we perceive as a delay in Jesus' second coming is our limited understanding of what God wants His people to achieve before Jesus returns. So let's get on our knees and ask God to expand our vision and bless us with His Spirit, and then let's roll up our sleeves and get to work so we can go home!

---

1. Ellen G. White, *Life Sketches of Ellen G. White* (Mountain View, CA: Pacific Press®, 1915), 125; emphasis added.

2. See P. Gerard Damsteegt, *Foundations of the Seventh-day Adventist Message and Mission* (Berrien Springs, MI: Andrews University Press, 1988), 75.

3. Ellen G. White, *Early Writings* (Battle Creek, MI: Review and Herald, 1882), 75.

4. James White, "Call at the Harbinger Office," *Review and Herald,* Feb. 17, 1852, 95.

5. Damsteegt, 281, citing Joseph Bates's letter to James White, *Review and Herald,* May 29, 1855, 240.

6. See Damsteegt, 281, 282.

7. I obtained much of the information for this section from volume 4 of Arthur W. Spalding's *Origin and History of Seventh-day Adventists* (Washington, DC: Review and Herald®, 1962), 41–70.

8. Ibid., 4:60.

9. The global membership of the Seventh-day Adventist Church at the end of each calendar year is listed in the church's annual statistical report, which is available at http://www.adventistarchives.org/documents.asp?CatID=11&SortBy=2&ShowDateOrder=True. Click on Annual Statistical Reports; then click on the report for each year to download it.

10. "1000 Days of Reaping: 121st Annual [Seventh-day Adventist] Statistical Report 1983," 2, http://www.adventistarchives.org/docs/ASR/ASR1983__B.pdf#view=fit.

11. Ibid.

12. Ibid.

13. "128th Annual Statistical Report—1990," 2, http://www.adventistarchives.org/docs/ASR/ASR1990__B.pdf#view=fit.

14. http://en.wikipedia.org/wiki/10/40_Window.

15. http://www.afmonline.org/about/index.php.

16. http://www.flyawa.org/article.php?id=441.

17. http://goaim.org/we/.

18. See http://www.maranatha.org and click on the link "About Us," then "What We Do," and "History."

PART 2

The Delay Is Almost Over

CHAPTER 6

Is Jesus *Really* Coming Soon?

Back in the 1940s, the Irish dramatist and poet Samuel Beckett wrote a play titled *Waiting for Godot*. The play tells the story of two homeless men who sit on the side of a road, waiting for a man by the name of Godot, who they suppose has promised to help them. The men keep waiting and waiting, but Godot never shows up. Some people believe Beckett's point to be that Christians have been waiting for Jesus to show up for the past two thousand years, but so far He hasn't—and, so this interpretation of the play goes, as far as Beckett is concerned, He won't.

Certainly, skeptics scoff at Christians who believe in Jesus' promised return. They say, "You Christians are foolish! You've been looking for the second coming of Jesus for millenniums, and He still hasn't showed up! Why don't you just give it all up as so much 'pie in the sky'?"

I propose that this is in fact a significant question. Two thousand years have gone by, so what reason do we Christians have for still believing that Jesus will show up in the clouds someday? After reading the previous three chapters, you're probably beginning to wonder why the editor of *Signs of the Times*® is raising all these questions about the Second Coming. Does Marvin Moore doubt the truth that lies behind the word *Adventist* in our name *Seventh-day Adventists*?

I want to assure you that I truly do believe in the nearness of Christ's second coming. I would never have allowed myself to become the editor of *Signs of the Times®* back in 1994 had I disagreed with this foundational teaching of our church—nor would I even have been offered the job! In this chapter, I will share with you the basis for my confidence in the soon return of Jesus.

Beliefs and authority

Every belief we humans hold is based on some authority. Children grow up believing in the tooth fairy and Santa Claus because of what they're told by their parents, grandparents, aunts, and uncles, and so on. At some point, of course, they learn that these are simply fantasies that people tell children and in fact they aren't true. Nevertheless, children still believe some things, and these beliefs are also based on what various authorities say. As children grow up and go to school, they learn that the world is round, that New York is located on the East Coast of the United States, and that a man named Julius Caesar ruled the Roman Empire some two thousand years ago. They, and we, believe these things on the authority of science, geography, and history. We've learned to trust these authorities, and we rely on them to help us make a myriad of decisions about life.

Why do we trust science, geography, and history? Because our five senses and our reasoning tell us they are reliable. Scientific observation has verified millions of details about our world. The knowledge that the world is round was first demonstrated conclusively several hundred years ago when a man named Magellan set out from Europe sailing west and kept sailing west till he came back to where he started. Today, photographic images from satellites provide even greater evidence that the world is round.

We know that New York City is located on the East Coast of the United States because of the maps that have been provided for us by cartographers. Many of us have used these maps to travel to New York City ourselves, and we know the city's location from personal observation. As for Julius Caesar, we believe he ruled the Roman Empire because specialists in the study of archaeology and ancient documents tell us about him and what he did.

Here's the key question of this book: on the basis of what authority do we believe in the second coming of Christ? Could it be that, like the stories of the tooth fairy and Santa Claus, the story of His return is a fraudulent fantasy?

As I said earlier, every belief must be based on some authority; otherwise, it's mere superstition at best and a tragic lie at worst. So, on what authority do we Christians base our belief, our certainty, in Christ's return, and what makes us sure He'll return soon?

Beliefs and assumptions

I'm going to say something that will seem to contradict what I've affirmed in the previous couple of pages: Some of our beliefs are based on assumptions for which there may be evidence, but which our five senses can't confirm. One assumption that philosophers debate is that there is such a thing as reality. Does matter really exist, or do we just think it does? Do we humans really exist, or do we merely think we do? And what is perception anyway? These questions may sound foolish, but philosophers consider them worthy of debate.

Let's get a bit less esoteric. How do we know that the world orbits the sun and that it rotates on its axis? Well, you say, because scientific evidence tells us so. Astronomers train their telescopes on the universe, and the evidence they find proves that the earth orbits the sun and turns on its axis. True enough. But several hundred years ago most people were certain that the earth was the center of the solar system and that the sun orbited the earth. After all, didn't the sun rise in the morning, cross the sky during the day, and set in the evening?

We now know that a false assumption—that something must be true because it appears (literally!) to be so—lay behind the idea that the earth is the center of the solar system. Nevertheless, we continue to assume that over time, our observations, while sometimes flawed, can lead us to increasing knowledge about reality.

The best assumptions are based on a combination of what we observe and certain conclusions we can draw from those assumptions that lie outside of our ability to demonstrate them by observation.

Now, to bring this theoretical discussion down to its practical conclusion: I propose that our belief in Christ's soon coming is based on an authority that itself is based on two key assumptions. If our two assumptions are correct, then the authority is trustworthy and Christ *will* return.

What are these two assumptions? First, that there is a God; and second, that He has revealed Himself in the Bible.

Assumption 1: There is a God. Hebrews 11:6 says that "anyone who comes to [God] must *believe* that he exists" (emphasis added). No one can prove scientifically that God exists, but neither can any atheist prove scientifically that He doesn't. However, there is strong evidence to support our belief in God.

The former atheist Antony Flew wrote a book that has a clever title. The words *There Is No God* are on the front cover of the book, but the word *No* has been crossed out and the word *A* has been inserted above it, so that it now reads *There Is a God*.[1] The book's subtitle makes it all clear. It says, *How the World's Most Notorious Atheist Changed His Mind*. The jacket of the book calls the author "a renowned philosopher who was arguably the best-known atheist in the English-speaking world until his announcement in 2004 that he now accepts the existence of God."

What led Antony Flew to change his mind? Here are his own words:

It's simply inconceivable that any material matrix or field can generate agents who think and act. Matter cannot produce conceptions [ideas] and perceptions. A force does not plan or think. So at the level of reason and everyday experience, we become immediately aware that the world of living, conscious, thinking beings has to originate in a living Source, a Mind.[2]

Flew's testimony is evidence of the truthfulness of the apostle Paul's words that "since the creation of the world God's invisible qualities—his eternal power and divine nature—have been clearly seen, being understood from what has been made" (Romans 1:20). This is why I make no apologies for the Christian assumption that there is a God. While we can't prove God's existence by observing Him, the evidence for His existence is too powerful to be ignored.

Assumption 2: God has revealed Himself in the Bible. Again, I can't prove to you scientifically that God inspired the Bible. But again, there are powerful evidences. I will mention what to me are the two strongest. The first is the power the Bible has to change the lives of the people who follow its counsel. A good example is Quirino, an Indian from the Amazon jungle who at first bitterly opposed the work of Leo and Jessie Halliwell. When the Halliwells appointed a couple as teachers at a school they had established among the Maues Indians, Quirino tried repeatedly to kill the teachers. Fortunately, he never succeeded.

Eventually, the Halliwells hired Quirino to be their guide as they ventured up the Amazon River and its tributaries. One night as they were chugging along, Mrs. Halliwell began singing the Portuguese song "Christ Saves Sinners." When she was through, Quirino asked Elder Halliwell to have her sing the song again, which she did. Then he asked her to sing it a third time. After she sang it again, Quirino was quiet for a while, and then he turned to Elder Halliwell and asked, "Do you think Jesus died to save the Indians too, or only white men?" Elder Halliwell replied, "Oh, Jesus died to save all sinners, including Indians!" And that night, Quirino, a hardened criminal who had killed six men, became a disciple of Jesus Christ.[3]

Conversions like this have taken place countless times throughout Christian history. I consider them to be powerful evidence that the Bible's message is true, for no merely human document can produce the kind of change in people's lives that the Bible does.

A second reason why I believe God inspired the Bible is that its prophecies have been fulfilled so accurately. I especially find this to be the case with the prophecies in Daniel 2 and 7. You're familiar, I'm sure, with King Nebuchadnezzar's dream of a great image with its head of gold, arms and chest of silver, abdomen of bronze, legs of iron, and feet of iron and clay. Daniel explained to the king that these metals represented four great empires that would arise in the world, the first of which was Nebuchadnezzar's own Babylon. We now know that the next three kingdoms were Media-Persia, Greece, and Rome, and the feet of iron and clay represent the nations of Europe that emerged after the break-up of the Roman Empire. The four beasts of Daniel 7—a lion, a bear, a leopard, and a dragon—represent the same four kingdoms, and the ten horns on the dragon's head represent the nations of Europe that emerged out of Rome. An additional symbol in chapter 7 is a religio-political "little horn" that the prophecy said would rise up among the other ten horns. We now identify that little horn as the medieval papacy.

Secular and liberal Christian interpreters claim that Daniel wrote his prophecies in the mid-second century B.C., when the Greeks still ruled, but Rome was growing strong. These skeptical interpreters conclude that at the time Daniel wrote the prophecies in his book, he didn't need divine revelation to know what would become of them because each of the four kingdoms either had already ruled, was now ruling, or quite obviously would rule in the future.

Let's assume for the moment that the critics are correct, that Daniel wrote his prophecies in the mid-second century B.C., at a time when he would have known about the four kingdoms. The question is, Why wouldn't a Daniel writing in 165 B.C. have predicted that Rome would be followed by a fifth kingdom? How did he know that Rome would be followed, not by a fifth kingdom, but by a multitude of kingdoms? From the perspective of a writer in the second century B.C., a fifth kingdom would have been more logical, since that's the way it had worked with all the preceding kingdoms. And how could the writer have known that a religio-political power would arise among those kingdoms? These are very reasonable questions for which there is no answer other than that Daniel received his information directly from God, whether in the second century B.C. or the sixth.

This, to me, is powerful evidence that God is the ultimate Author of the Bible and that He really did inspire its human authors. This is why I make no apology for the conservative Christian assumptions that there *is* a God and that He has revealed Himself in the Old and New Testaments.

These two assumptions are the starting point for the Adventist confidence in the nearness of Christ's return. But, in themselves, they don't respond to the critics who say that we are foolish to think Jesus is coming at all, nor do they tell us that His return is near. So let's discuss these two issues.

Christ is coming

My first reason for believing that *Jesus will come someday* is simply that He promised that He would. "Do not let your hearts be troubled," He said.

> "You believe in God; believe also in me. My Father's house has many rooms; if that were not so, would I have told you that I am going there to prepare a place for you? And if I go and prepare a place for you, *I will come back and take you to be with me that you also may be where I am*" (John 14:1–3; emphasis added).

I believe Jesus will come again someday simply because He promised to return, and His promise is recorded in the Bible, which I accept as true.

The angels who spoke to Jesus' disciples at the time of His ascension made a similar promise. " 'Men of Galilee,' they said, 'why do you stand here looking into the sky? This same Jesus, who has been taken from you into heaven, *will come back in the same way you have seen him go into heaven*' " (Acts 1:11; emphasis added). Paul assured the Christians in Thessalonica that "the Lord himself will come down from heaven, with a loud command, with the voice of the archangel and with the trumpet call of God" (1 Thessalonians 4:16).

We find the same promise throughout the New Testament. James, for instance, said, "The Lord's coming is near" (James 5:8). While he misunderstood *when* Christ would return, he assured us that He *will* return. And writing in the book of Revelation, John said, " 'Look, he is coming with clouds,' and 'every eye will see him' " (Revelation 1:7).

So either Jesus is wrong, and the entire New Testament is wrong, or else the Bible is God's inspired Word and we can trust its promise of Christ's return regardless of how long it's been since He made the promise.

His return is near

If two thousand years have passed since the apostles believed Jesus' return was near, and if more than 160 years have passed since our Adventist pioneers believed Jesus' return was near, what reason have we to believe that today His second coming *really is near*? I will suggest two reasons.

The timeline of Daniel's prophecies. Daniel told King Nebuchadnezzar that the fourth kingdom, the Roman Empire, would be followed by a number of smaller states, represented by the feet of iron and clay. In the king's dream, a stone struck the image on its feet, knocking it down, and then the stone ground the image into a powder that the wind blew away. According to Daniel, this meant that "in the time of those kings [the nations of divided Europe], the God of heaven will set up a kingdom that will never be destroyed. . . . It will crush all those kingdoms and bring them to an end, but it [God's kingdom] will itself endure forever" (Daniel 2:44). Adventists have always understood the stone striking the image to represent the second coming of Jesus.

The empires of Babylon, Media-Persia, Greece, and Rome have all come and gone. We live in the time of the divided Europe. In fact, in our day the whole world is fractured into more than two hundred political entities that are continually fighting each other—if not with bullets, then with words.

The point is this: *the second coming of Jesus is the very next thing the king's dream pictured happening.* And because the part of the dream about Babylon, Media-Persia, Greece, Rome, and divided Europe has been fulfilled so exactly, we can be sure that the final event will also happen on schedule.

The vision of Daniel recorded in chapter 7 gives us even more detail about these kingdoms and end-time events. Daniel said that he saw four great beasts arise from the sea—a lion, a bear, a leopard, and a dragon. These beasts represent the same powers as did the metals in chapter 2. The fourth beast, the dragon, had ten horns on its head, representing the nations of divided Europe. In the dream, a little horn popped up among the ten horns, and Daniel's angel interpreter said the power it represented would blaspheme God, persecute His saints, and attempt to change His laws. We understand this little horn to represent the medieval papacy. The very next event pictured in Daniel's vision was the handing over of the kingdoms of the world to the Son of Man and His saints.

Again, we know that Babylon, Media-Persia, Greece, and Rome have come and gone, as has the medieval papacy.* In other words, nearly everything this vision pictured as happening before earth's last days has already happened just as Daniel foretold it. And if everything else in Daniel's vision has been fulfilled exactly as he predicted it, then we can be sure that the final event—the second coming of Jesus—will also happen, and soon, because it's the very next item on the agenda!

Daniel's time prophecies. More than two thousand years ago, the seventy-week prophecy of Daniel 9 provided God's people with information by which they could have known that the Messiah's first coming was near. God also gave Daniel two time prophecies by which we today can know that Christ's second coming is near.

The first of these two time prophecies is the 1,260 days of Daniel 7:25. According to the year-day principle, 1,260 *days* represent 1,260 *years*.† These 1,260 years began in A.D. 538, and they ended in 1798, which is exactly when the medieval papacy fell.‡ Since the next major event on planet Earth following Daniel's 1,260-year prophecy is the second coming of Jesus, we can know that ever since 1798, His return has been about to happen.

The second time prophecy is the 2,300 days—or years—of Daniel 8:14. This prophecy is much too involved to explain here;§ I'll just tell you that Adventists understand these 2,300 "days" (in the text, "evenings-mornings," which means "days") to have begun in 457 B.C. and ended in A.D. 1844. This vision was even more specific than Daniel's previous visions had been. In it, Gabriel tells Daniel that the vision "con-

---

* The papacy is still very much with us, but not in its medieval form.

† I give a detailed explanation of the year-day principle in chapter 27 of my book *The Case for the Investigative Judgment.*

‡ I give a detailed explanation of the beginning and end of the 1,260 years in chapter 4 of my book *Could It* Really *Happen?*

§ In chapters 16 and 25 of my book, *The Case for the Investigative Judgment,* I give a detailed explanation of the beginning and end dates of the 2,300-day prophecy.

cerns the time of the end" (verse 17; see also verse 19). If the 2,300 days ended in 1844, then the time of the end began at that time and continues to this day.* Jesus' second coming marks the end of time, and the time of the end is the period immediately prior to His return.

So is Jesus coming soon? Absolutely! Ever since 1844, it's been appropriate for God's people to say so. I realize that the 160-plus years since 1844 sounds like a long time to us because even if we're lucky and we take care of our health, we live only about half that long. However, in the span of human history, 160 years is a very short time. And it most certainly is a short time for God, the Ancient of Days. That's why I don't hesitate to tell you that *Jesus is coming soon!*

And there's more. Much more. Current events tell me that Jesus is coming soon. Adventists often refer to these indicators as "signs" of Christ's soon return. In the next five chapters, I will share with you five signs that tell me the Second Coming truly is near.

---

1. Antony Flew, *There Is a God: How the World's Most Notorious Atheist Changed His Mind* (New York: HarperOne, 2007).

2. Ibid., 183.

3. See Spalding, *Origin and History of Seventh-day Adventists,* 4:55, 56.

---

* Please note that there's a difference between the "time of the end" and the "end of time."

CHAPTER 7

A Sign of the End:
The Gospel to All the World

Canaanite slave workers in the turquoise mines of the Sinai Peninsula invented alphabet writing in the secound millennium before Christ, probably only a short time before Moses wrote Genesis. This brought about a rapid advance in human communication. In the second millennium after Christ—about 1455—Johannes Gutenberg invented movable type and the printing press, and this brought about another rapid advance in human communication. Most important for our study, Gutenberg's invention made possible the launching of the Protestant Reformation. It's doubtful that the Reformation could have happened the way it did without the printing press.

How the Reformation got started

The Reformation was sparked by the effort of Leo X to raise money for the renovation of St. Peter's Basilica in Rome. In the year 1517, the pope authorized a man by the name of Johann Tetzel, a Dominican priest, to sell indulgences* in Germany. The archbishop of Mainz, who had borrowed a tidy sum to pay for his appointment, was to receive a cut of the proceeds.

At that time, Martin Luther was a Catholic priest and a professor of

---

* In Roman Catholic theology, an indulgence is the full or partial remission of temporal punishment due for sins that have been forgiven.

theology at the University of Wittenberg. He occasionally heard confession of sins from parishioners in that city. He was outraged when some of those who came to him for confession presented the indulgences they had bought from Tetzel and said they'd been told they didn't have to do any more penances for their sins because the indulgences covered them.

Luther was totally opposed to the church's practice of selling indulgences, so he proposed a public meeting in which some of the scholars at his university could debate what the church was doing. He wrote up a series of "theses"—propositions—for the debate; and on October 31, 1517, he nailed them to the church door in Wittenberg,* which had become something of a bulletin board where people posted all kinds of notices.[1]

Luther's proposal, which has come to be known as the Ninety-five Theses, was written in Latin, not German. However, someone copied it and translated it into the German language. By this time, printing presses had been established all over Europe, and whoever translated Luther's document had it printed. It spread like wildfire. Within two weeks, it had been distributed all over Germany, and within two months, it had been translated into the various languages of Europe and spread all over the continent![2] By the time the church caught on to what was happening, it was too late to stop it.

The Catholic Church opposed Luther bitterly, but he continued preaching and writing against the papal system of righteousness by works. In June 1520, the pope wrote a bull[†] titled *Exsurge Domine* ("Arise, O Lord"), in which he warned Luther that unless he recanted his teachings he would be excommunicated. Luther responded by publicly burning the pope's bull. So, in early January 1521, Leo X issued a bull that officially excommunicated Luther. The following April, Luther appeared

---

* Luther's nailing the Ninety-five Theses to the church door in Wittenberg is a story with a long tradition. That Luther wrote these propositions is quite well accepted in scholarly circles, but some scholars question whether Luther actually nailed them to the church door. The story comes from a statement made by his associate Philipp Melanchthon, in 1546—nearly twenty years after the fact.

† An official public document issued by a pope.

before the Diet* of Worms to answer the papal charge of heresy. It was on this occasion that he made the famous statement, "Unless I am convinced by the testimony of Scripture or by the clearest reasoning, . . . I cannot and I will not retract, for it is unsafe for a Christian to speak against his conscience. May God help me. Amen."† With that, the Reformation was in full swing.

The role of the printing press

It's critical that we understand that Luther didn't set out to start a reformation. His only purpose in posting his Ninety-five Theses was to start a discussion among the scholars at the University of Wittenberg. Probably no one was more surprised than he at the rapid unfolding of events. Today's students of Luther's life attribute the speed with which his document was circulated to social unrest, especially the people's weariness with the heavy hand of the church, and I'm sure this was a factor, just as, fifteen hundred years earlier, political and social factors prepared the way for Christ's coming.‡ But the speed with which events unfolded after Luther posted his theses is clear evidence to me that God took Luther's initiative into His own hands.

And Gutenberg's invention had everything to do with it. The printing press, after all, is simply a device for making information quickly available to many people for a reasonable price. Prior to Gutenberg's printing press, it generally took a scribe a year or more to produce a single copy of the Bible, tediously writing it out a word at a time by hand. If this had been the only means of disseminating information in Luther's day, it would have been impossible for word of his challenge to the Roman Church to have spread as rapidly as it did. But the printing press provided a mechanical way to produce hundreds of copies in a matter of weeks. To us, that's a snail's pace. We're accustomed to publishing houses that can produce hundreds of thousands of copies of the Bible in a

---

* The word *diet* in this sense is a formal assembly, a hearing, a council meeting.

† Luther has been quoted as also saying, "Here I stand. I can do no other." However, current scholarship considers the evidence that he said this to be unreliable.

‡ See, for example, Ellen G. White, *The Desire of Ages,* 32.

matter of days. But back then, a few hundred copies in a few weeks was revolutionary. *And it came just in time to push the Reformation into fast-forward.*

John Wycliffe tried to reform the church in the mid-1300s. It didn't work. Huss and Jerome tried to reform the church in the 1400s, and so did Girolamo Savonarola. It didn't work. Along came Martin Luther in the early 1500s, and he had no thought of starting a reformation, but it took off and dragged him along with it.

I propose that God led Gutenberg to invent the printing press in 1455 so that by 1517 it could grow a full-blown reformation from Luther's Ninety-five Theses, even though that was the last thing he had on his mind. God has ways of transforming our simple actions into powerful tools for the advancement of His kingdom!

Today's technology

Now let's look at the technology God has placed in our hands during the past 150 years.

Telephones. In March 1876, the United States Patent Office awarded Alexander Graham Bell patent number 174,465 for "Improvement in Telegraphy." His invention was a device that could transmit voices over an electric wire. We today call it the telephone. By early in the twentieth century, telephones were in fairly wide use in the United States. However, I can still remember back in the 1950s having to dial up an operator in order to place a long-distance call. AT&T introduced the touch-tone telephone in the 1960s. Today, anyone can dial any telephone number in the world by simply pressing a dozen or so keys on the touch pad of his or her phone. And the cost of long-distance calls has dropped dramatically. Back in the 1950s, because of the cost, few people called long distance even within the United States. Today, I can enter a number for a person or a business in Australia, and less than a minute later, the party at the other end of the line answers. And with the right phone card, the cost is about three cents per minute!

Then there are cell phones, which have changed the way of life for millions not only in the Western nations but in third-world countries.

My wife and I have visited India numerous times in the past few years to conduct evangelistic meetings in rural villages, and many of the people in these villages have cell phones. The advantage of the cell phone is that it doesn't require a land line. Instead, it transmits a radio signal to a nearby tower, and with a network of towers, people can make and receive calls anywhere in the world. The first hand-held cell phone was demonstrated by Martin Cooper of Motorola in 1973. It weighed 2.5 pounds! Many of today's cell phones weigh less than four ounces. In 1990, 12.4 million people worldwide had cell phones. By the beginning of 2010, 4.6 billion people around the world were using cell phones![3]

The telephone is an amazing technological development.

Radio. The Italian inventor Guglielmo Marconi has been credited with inventing the radio, though during the last quarter of the nineteenth century, many people were experimenting with wireless communication, including Thomas Edison. Marconi's fame arises from the fact that he was the first person to transmit a radio signal across the Atlantic Ocean. By 1912, radio transmission was being widely used by ships at sea to communicate with their land-based headquarters. When the *Titanic* sank in the North Atlantic Ocean on April 2, 1912, radio technology enabled nearby ships to go to the aid of the stricken vessel, though they arrived too late to save the more than fifteen hundred passengers who died.

Today, hundreds of radio stations around the world transmit programming to nearly all of the world's seven billion people. Adventist World Radio (AWR) operates transmitters in eight countries* that broadcast short-wave programs, and it also broadcasts on more than seventy FM stations in Africa and the Americas. In addition, AWR produces programs for podcasts and the Internet. All together, AWR broadcasts programming in one hundred languages.

The radio is an amazing technological development.

Television. The first person to create a system for transmitting images telegraphically was a Scottish inventor by the name of Alexander Bain,

---

* AWR owns a transmitter in Guam, and it rents transmitters in Germany, Austria, France, Poland, South Africa, Madagascar, and Taiwan.

who did so back in the 1840s. However, it wasn't until the 1920s that John Baird, also a Scotsman, invented a device to transmit moving images. Baird is generally considered to be the actual inventor of television as we know it today.

While commercially made television sets were first marketed in the late 1920s and early 1930s, it was not until the late 1940s and early 1950s that they came into widespread use in the developed countries of the world. Today, people in New York, Toronto, and Los Angeles can sit in front of large flat-screen TVs hanging on the walls in their living rooms and watch a reporter in Sydney, Australia, give a live, running commentary about something that's happening there! We take this technology for granted, but it's truly astounding.

Television is an amazing technological development.

Air travel. The brothers Orville and Wilbur Wright are credited with inventing the first airplane that actually flew. Orville made the first successful flight on December 17, 1903. His plane covered 120 feet in 12 seconds at a speed of 6.8 miles per hour. Other flights that day extended the distance to 175 feet and then 200 feet and reached the height of 10 feet above the ground. Today, the world's largest commercial airliner, the Airbus A380-800, is designed to ferry up to 850 people at a top speed of 650 miles per hour for almost 8,500 miles nonstop in about fifteen hours!

I grew up in Latin America, where my parents were missionaries for many years. We lived in Argentina for seven years, and then, in June 1949, we returned to the United States for a one-year furlough. Our ship sailed from Buenos Aires and made stops in Montevideo, Sao Paulo, Rio de Janeiro, and Trinidad. The trip took two weeks—a nice cruise, courtesy of the General Conference! Today's missionaries rarely have the privilege of such a cruise. Within ten years of that boat trip with my parents, jet passenger service had been established to most parts of the world, and ever since, most missionaries leaving their homeland arrive at their destination within twenty-four to forty-eight hours.

My wife and I have traveled from the United States to India numerous times on three-week evangelistic trips. This would have been very difficult prior to about 1960, because just the trip there and back could take a couple of weeks or more. But now, because the travel time has been so drastically decreased, thousands of short-term missionaries leave their homelands for stints as short as a week in the remotest parts of the world, and furloughs back home for those missionaries who stay for longer stretches of service typically last just one or two months. In the late 1800s and early 1900s, it was very common for business trips made by early Adventist leaders to the church's outposts in foreign lands to require six months or more away from home. Today, church leaders from North America can travel to a meeting in Europe, Asia, Africa, or Latin America, spend a day or two, or perhaps a week, and then return to their offices and their families.

Global air travel is an amazing technological development.

The Internet. If time should last long enough, I suspect that the Internet will be listed as being as significant an invention as writing and printing. It is already transforming the way we communicate with each other and the way we do business.

E-mail. The Internet began in the 1960s as a way for the United States military to connect its computers at the Pentagon with the major command centers at Cheyenne Mountain near Colorado Springs, Colorado, and the Strategic Air Command in Omaha, Nebraska.[4] This electronic communication between two or more parties has developed into what is now called e-mail, and it continues to be one of the two major uses of the Internet today. In the very early stages, computer operators at each end of the communication exchange had to be logged on at the same time. Today, anyone with a computer and an e-mail address can send a message to anyone else in the world who has a computer and an e-mail address, regardless of whether or not their computers are connected to the Internet at the same time.

The Web. The British computer scientist Tim Berners-Lee is credited with inventing the World Wide Web in 1989. The Web has transformed the way people do business. Two of the best-known online sellers are eBay and Amazon. e-Bay enables people to sell almost anything online* through a bidding process.

---

* The company has strict rules regarding the sale of certain items, such as alcohol, tobacco, drugs, sexual products, and firearms.

Jeff Bezos started Amazon in 1994, naming his company after the world's largest river. At first, Amazon sold only books, but today it sells a wide variety of products. In 2010, it was second only to Wal-Mart in annual sales.[5]

The Internet has also had a major impact on the way the Adventist Church and other religious organizations do their business. Certain communications still must be sent by postal mail, but I think I'm safe in saying that by far the majority of communications between church entities today is done by e-mail.

A case in point is *Signs of the Times*®, of which I am the editor. Since January 2007, we have cooperated with the Australian *Signs of the Times*® in the production of our two magazines. We share certain articles each month, and each edition also has its own unique articles, columns, and departments. Our offices are half a world apart, but we keep in close touch with each other through e-mail and phone calls. Sometimes, as we're talking on the phone, one of us will send an e-mail to the other, and the e-mail will reach the other's inbox while we are still on the phone.

The Australian editor, Lee Dunstan, and his associate, Melody Tan, send me the articles they're providing as e-mail attachments, and I edit them to conform to American English, grammar, units of measure (such as miles instead of kilometers), and so on. When I have finished editing all of the articles for a given issue (both those I provide and those that Australia has provided), I send everything to Australia as an e-mail attachment, and their designer, Shane Winfield, lays out the magazine. He sends the initial layout back to my office as an e-mail attachment in a low-resolution format, and the proofreaders and I read the entire issue carefully, making corrections where needed. I phone the Australian designer with these corrections, and when, after several back-and-forth versions, my proofreaders and I are satisfied that everything is in order, the Australian designer sends a final high-resolution version of the issue to Pacific Press® over the Internet, and we print it here in the United States.

The Internet, e-mail, and the World Wide Web are amazing technological developments.

The point I'm making is that none of this would have been possible as recently as 1995 or even 2000. And *Signs of the Times*® is just one small example of the way Christians around the world, including Seventh-day Adventists, are using the Internet today for the advancement of the gospel.

A sign of the end

The most specific sign of the end in the entire Bible is Jesus' statement that the "gospel of the kingdom will be preached in the whole world as a testimony to all nations, and then the end will come" (Matthew 24:14). Jesus didn't say that everyone will *accept* the gospel; He only said that everyone in the world must hear—must be exposed in one way or another—to the gospel. When that objective has been reached, then He will return. The problem, of course, is that you and I won't know when that milestone has been reached. Only God will know when every human being on planet Earth has had an opportunity to hear or read the gospel.

However, I propose that beginning in the second half of the nineteenth century, God began placing in human hands the means to proclaim the gospel much more rapidly. And during the twentieth century He especially placed radio and television at our disposal, including the opportunity, through satellite technology, for an evangelist in one place on the globe to preach a sermon that can be heard and seen live anywhere else in the world. Adventist World Radio is making it possible for people in Africa, Asia, and Latin America to hear the gospel in their own languages, especially in countries that discourage or ban Christian evangelism. Adventist World Aviation is carrying the gospel to people in the remotest parts of the planet who can't travel outside their small part of the world. And the Adventist Development and Relief Agency is doing all kinds of humanitarian work in the underdeveloped parts of the world.

We don't know when the gospel will have been preached to the whole world. What we do know is that just as God brought a quantum leap forward in printing technology to jump-start the Reformation five hundred years ago, so He has given His church today the technology to finish the proclamation of the gospel on a global scale practically overnight.

Back in the first decade of the twentieth century, Ellen White said, "The final movements will be rapid ones."[6] The Holy Spirit will most certainly be a part of that process, but He will work through people—people who are using our modern methods of communication and travel to accomplish the task far more rapidly than would have been possible in Ellen White's day. This, to me, is a powerful sign that *the delay in Christ's return is nearing its end.*

And there are other signs!

---

1. For a list of the Ninety-five Theses, see http://www.iclnet.org/pub/resources/text/wittenberg/luther/web/ninetyfive.html.

2. See http://en.wikipedia.org/wiki/Martin_Luther.

3. See http://en.wikipedia.org/wiki/Cell_phone.

4. See http://en.wikipedia.org/wiki/Internet#History.

5. See http://en.wikipedia.org/wiki/Amazon.com#History.

6. Ellen G. White, *Testimonies for the Church* (Nampa, ID: Pacific Press®, 1948), 9:11.

CHAPTER 8

A Sign of the End: Spiritualism

Joanne—she preferred being called just Jo—worked as a researcher and bilingual secretary for Amnesty International in London. When she and her boyfriend decided to move to Manchester, about two hundred miles from London, they spent a weekend hunting for an apartment. On their return trip, Jo got a sudden inspiration for a novel. She spent the entire trip imagining the plot, and the moment she got home she started writing. It took several years, but she eventually finished the manuscript and then started looking for an agent to help her get it published. The first one turned her down, but the second one called and said Yes. Yet even the agent had a hard time finding a publisher. Finally, on the twelfth try, he found one that also said Yes. Jo was so shocked when her agent called with the news that as soon as she hung up, she started screaming and jumping up and down![1] Jo was a single mom on welfare at the time. Five years later, she was a billionaire.

In case you haven't guessed it by now, the title of her first novel, published in 1997, is *Harry Potter and the Philosopher's Stone* (*Harry Potter and the Sorcerer's Stone* in the United States), and Jo is better known as J. K. Rowling. Six more Harry Potter novels followed that first one. The fourth book, *Harry Potter and the Goblet of Fire,* was released on July 8, 2000. In the United States, it sold three million copies in the first forty-eight hours, breaking all literary sales records. Yet that was just the beginning. Each of the next three books broke the sales records of the previous ones. Rowling's last book, *Harry Potter and the Deathly Hollows,* released on July 7, 2007, sold eleven million copies in the United States and Britain during the first twenty-four hours!

Then there's Stephenie Meyer, author of *Twilight* and its three successors, *New Moon, Eclipse,* and *Breaking Dawn.*[2] Meyer, a devout Mormon, grew up in Phoenix, Arizona, one of six children.[3] The night of June 2, 2003, she had a vivid dream about a girl and "a fantastically beautiful, sparkly vampire." She woke up with the dream still vivid in her mind, so as soon as she'd finished her morning chores, she sat down at her computer and wrote down as much of the dream as she could remember. For the next three months, she wrote every day, mostly when her children were in bed. As she finished each chapter, she shared it with her sister Emily.

When Emily had read the entire manuscript, she suggested that Meyer try to get it published. With great fear and trepidation, Meyer wrote queries to fifteen agents. Five never responded, and nine said no, but an assistant at Writers House asked to see the first three chapters. A few weeks later, Meyer received a letter asking for the entire manuscript. At that point she also did a lot of screaming! Four weeks after that an agent called asking to represent her. By November, Meyer had signed a $750,000 contract with Little, Brown and Company to publish the book.

The initial print run of *Twilight* was seventy-five thousand copies. Within a month of its release, it had reached number five on the *New York Times* bestseller list for children's chapter books, and it eventually rose to number one. *Publisher's Weekly* named it "Best Book of the Year." *New Moon,* the second book in the series, hit the number-one spot on the *New York Times* bestseller list for children's chapter books in just one week. The initial print run for *Breaking Dawn,* the fourth book in the series, was 3.7 million copies; more than 1.3 million sold on the first day of its release! In 2008, Meyer's books sold more than 29 million copies. By early 2010, the series had been translated into at least thirty-eight languages and had sold more than 100 million copies worldwide. Meyer was the bestselling author in both 2008 and 2009, and the four Twilight books were in the top ten on *USA Today*'s bestseller list for fifty-two weeks, breaking J. K. Rowling's record. In 2010, *Forbes* reported Meyer's annual earnings at forty million dollars.

Twilight—a film version of the first book—has been a blockbuster moneymaker for Summit Entertainment, the studio that produced it. On its release date, November 21, 2008, it grossed $35.7 million, and it nearly doubled that ($70.2 million) the first weekend. By April 2009, it had brought in $380 million worldwide and $127 million in DVD sales. As of this writing (December 2010), three of the books have been turned into film, and they have brought in $1.7 billion!

Why do I tell you these stories? What's the significance of these phenomenally successful novels? Both of them illustrate a stark truth: the occult is a hot commodity these days.

The basic plot: Spiritualism

Rowling's Harry Potter novels are about a boy with magical powers who is invited to attend Hogwarts School of Witchcraft and Wizardry, a boarding school for would-be witches and wizards ages eleven to eighteen. The basic plot is about Harry's conflict with the evil Lord Voldemort. This villain tries to kill Harry, but Harry uses magic arts and witchcraft to foil him. In the last book, Voldemort conjures a killing curse on Harry, who, near death, has an out-of-body encounter with his deceased mentor at Hogwarts, Professor Albus Dumbledore. The professor advises him on curses and spells he can use to thwart Voldemort, and Harry uses them to bring about the death of his evil antagonist.

The storyline of the Harry Potter series is a classic example of the universal theme of good against evil, which is also the theme of the Adventist concept of the great controversy. The problem lies in the fact that in the Harry Potter books, the good guys are witches and wizards just as the bad guys are.

The Twilight series is about a high school girl named Bella Swan who falls in love with a boy she spies at a table in her school cafeteria in Forks, Washington. As the story progresses, Bella discovers that Edward is a vampire who looks like a teen but is actually more than one hundred years old. He's obsessed with a desire to drink Bella's blood, though he restrains himself from actually doing so. They eventually fall in love, and she wants him to bite her and turn her into a vampire, too, but he refuses. Later, Bella falls in love with a character named Jacob, who can turn himself into a werewolf. However, she realizes that she loves Edward more than Jacob, and in the fourth book she and Edward get married. Shortly thereafter, she nearly dies while giving birth to a daughter who is half human and half vampire. To save her life, Edward injects her with his venom, turning her into the immortal vampire she had wanted to be ever since she learned he was a vampire.

The Harry Potter books have been especially popular with children, and the Twilight books have been popular with teens and young adults. Defenders of the books point out that they help children to develop an interest in reading, and both series have a moral theme in which good wins out over evil. Both of these claims are true, but the stories of both series are about witches and vampires, who are portrayed as real beings, and, as I said, *the good characters are witches and vampires just like the bad ones.* Stories have powerful influences on our minds, which is why Jesus did much of His teaching through stories, particularly parables. Most children can, of course, recognize that, like Santa Claus, witches and vampires aren't real. Nevertheless, *reading these books makes children susceptible to regarding witchcraft favorably.*

That's the point.

TV programs

During the mid-1960s and early 1970s the American fascination with witchcraft was enhanced by the TV sitcom *Bewitched.* The 1990s saw several major TV programs about witchcraft, including *Sabrina, the Teenage Witch, Buffy the Vampire Slayer,* and *Charmed.* In each series, the witches are portrayed as having high morals and using their magical powers to help human beings. *Charmed* garnered 7.7 million viewers for its first episode in October 1998, and it remained popular till the end—its last episode, in May 2006, being viewed by nearly 4.5 million people.

During the last half of the twentieth century, the occult also became popular among adults, with programs such as *Medium* and *Ghost Whisperer* filling slots on prime time TV. *Medium* began showing on the NBC network in January 2005, and, as of this writing, it is still being aired. The program is based on the life of Allison DuBois, a real-life medium, who claims to talk to dead people, foresee future events, and witness the past in her dreams. Early in the series, she takes a job as an intern with the Phoenix, Arizona, district attorney and has a dream about a murder in Texas that helps him solve the crime. As a result, he becomes convinced of her psychic abilities and uses her to help him solve other crimes.

Ghost Whisperer ran on the CBS network from September 2005 to May 2010. The show was about a woman named Melinda Gordon who was able to see and communicate with dead people. These ghosts, especially those whose consciences are troubling them about things they did while physically alive, are earthbound and therefore unable to "cross over into the light"—presumably heaven, though the show doesn't say so. They seek Melinda's aid, and, as their earthly representative, she helps them communicate with people who are still alive so the ghosts can wrap up business that they had left unresolved when they died. This relieves them of their guilt and fear of judgment so they can enter into a meaningful afterlife.

In addition to all of this, there are a couple of TV shows hosted by professed mediums John Edward and James Van Praagh. Edward's first program, *Crossing Over With John Edward,* ran from 1999 to 2004 on the SCI FI channel (which became the Syfy channel) in the United States and on LIVINGtv in the United Kingdom. Edward's current program, *John Edward Cross Country,* began airing on We TV in 2006, and, as of this writing, it is still going. In both programs, Edward claims to communicate with the deceased friends and relatives of people in his audience. In *Crossing Over,* Edward received information from the audience about the individuals they wished to contact, while in *Cross Country* he is not supposed to receive any prior information about the person or the family of the person he is supposed to contact. He simply " 'lets his guides draw him to the people that spirits are trying to connect with, and the audience should only validate the information he gives them.' "[4]

In 1995, James Van Praagh appeared on the NBC television program

The Other Side. He was the first medium to perform readings on the air and quickly became the series' favorite. During 2002 and 2003, he hosted a daytime talk show called *Beyond With James Van Praagh.* Following that, he teamed up with CBS to produce several movies and miniseries, including *Living With the Dead* and *The Dead Will Tell.* He was the coexecutive producer of the television series *Ghost Whisperer,* which I mentioned above.

Opinions differ about the authenticity of John Edward, James Van Praagh, Allison DuBois, and other mediums like them. Gary Schwartz, a graduate of Harvard University, is the director of a research program at the University of Arizona that tests the hypothesis that people's consciousnesses survive their physical deaths. He has tested John Edward and Allison DuBois, and based on his research, which he claims was done under controlled conditions, he has concluded that DuBois can indeed contact dead people. " 'There is no question this is not a fraud,' " he says. " 'Some people really can do this, and Allison is one of them.' "[5]

On the other hand, the skeptic James Randi calls such claims "woo-woo."[6] A former magician, Randi has turned to investigating claims of the paranormal, the occult, and the supernatural. His organization, the James Randi Educational Foundation (JREF), is dedicated to educating the public on the dangers of accepting unproven claims about life after death, the occult, and the supernatural. JREF also supports investigation into the paranormal under controlled conditions. The organization offers a prize of one million dollar to anyone who can demonstrate a paranormal or supernatural ability while meeting agreed-upon scientific criteria. He has offered this challenge to Allison DuBois but says that so far she has refused the invitation.

So, are Edward, Van Praagh, DuBois, and others like them genuine examples of spiritualism? Adventists and other Christians who believe that demonic forces can impersonate the dead through séances find it easy to believe that these modern examples of the occult are real. Skeptics find it easy to believe they are charades. For our purpose in this book, it doesn't really matter whether they do in fact communicate with the dead or not. What matters is that they are contributing to the acceptance of spiritualism in America, which is already very widespread and continues to grow.

Wicca

Then there's Wicca, a neo-pagan religion and a form of modern witchcraft that some people claim is the fastest growing religion in the United States, especially among high school and college students. Wiccans believe in fairies, spirits, gods, goddesses, and a spiritual life that is largely invisible to the average human. In the past, witches have been severely persecuted, especially by Christians. The Salem witch trials in 1692 and 1693 are probably the best-known examples in America. No Christian should countenance the persecution of witches; however, the connection of witches to the occult is obvious.

Wicca received a powerful boost in 1998 with the publication of the book *Teen Witch: Wicca for a New Generation* by Silver RavenWolf, who claims to be "one of the most famous Witches in the United States today."[7] The book's cover features five teens—a boy and four girls—in "cool" poses. RavenWolf closes the introduction, which she has written to parents, by saying, "If you feel that the Craft [witchcraft] is still against your belief system after you've read this book, don't panic. I've written this book so that your teen (or you) can take any of the techniques herein and use them in your own religious background."[8] In its March 1, 1999, issue, *U.S. News & World Report* called *Teen Witch*, "a 250-page handbook that is flying off the shelves at Borders, Barnes & Noble, and other mainstream stores. . . . It boasts everything a kid needs to become 'a pentacle-wearing, spell-casting, completely authentic witch!' That includes instructions for such uniquely teen rituals as the Bad Bus Driver spell, the Un-Ground Me spell, and the Just-Say-No spell."[9]

A sign of the end

How is all of this a sign of the end?

When Jesus was listing the signs that will indicate the nearness of His second coming, He warned that "false messiahs and false prophets will appear and perform great signs and wonders to deceive, if possible, even the elect" (Matthew 24:24). In the same vein, Paul predicted that at the very end of time, "The coming of the lawless one will be in accordance with how Satan works. He will use all sorts of displays of power through signs and wonders that serve the lie, and all the ways that wickedness deceives those who are perishing" (2 Thessalonians 2:9, 10). And writing in Revelation 16 about the seven last plagues, John said that he saw

> three impure spirits that looked like frogs; they came out of the mouth of the dragon, out of the mouth of the beast and out of the mouth of the false prophet. They are demonic spirits that perform signs, and they go out to the kings of the whole world, to gather them for the battle on the great day of God Almighty (verses 13, 14).

The point is that at the very end of time, spiritualism will be widespread. In fact, according to John, demonic forces will actually communicate with the world's great political leaders, uniting them into a powerful force for the purpose of destroying God's people and actually attempting to defeat Christ at His second coming (see Revelation 17:12–14; 19:19, 20).

Ellen White predicted,

> As the crowning act in the great drama of deception, Satan himself will personate Christ. . . . The great deceiver will make it appear that Christ has come. In different parts of the earth, Satan will manifest himself among men as a majestic being of dazzling brightness, resembling the description of the Son of God given by John in the Revelation. Revelation 1:13-15. The glory that surrounds him is unsurpassed by anything that mortal eyes have yet beheld. The shout of triumph rings out upon the air: "Christ has come! Christ has come!" The people prostrate themselves in adoration before him, while he lifts up his hands and pronounces a blessing upon them, as Christ blessed His disciples when He was upon the earth. His voice is soft and subdued, yet full of melody. . . . This is the strong, almost overmastering delusion.[10]

She also warned that "little by little [Satan] has prepared for his masterpiece of deception in the development of spiritualism. He has not yet reached the full accomplishment of his designs; but it will be reached in the last remnant of time."[11]

According to the Bible, spiritualism will be rampant in the end time. Harry Potter, the Twilight series, and the TV programs I have mentioned are catching the imaginations of millions of children, young people, and adults. And Wicca is adding to the trend. Note also that most of this has developed in America since about the mid-1990s. I propose to you that this is a powerful sign that the delay is almost over. This development provides God's people with another indication that we are living in the end time.

The delay in Christ's return is nearing its end.

1. J. K. Rowling Official Site, "Section: Biography," http://www.jkrowling.com /textonly/en/biography.cfm.

2. http://www.stepheniemeyer.com/twilight.html.

3. http://en.wikipedia.org/wiki/Stephenie_Meyer#Personal_life.

4. http://en.wikipedia.org/wiki/John_Edward.

5. http://en.wikipedia.org/wiki/Gary_Schwartz.

6. http://en.wikipedia.org/wiki/James_Randi.

7. Silver RavenWolf, *Teen Witch: Wicca for a New Generation* (St. Paul, MN: Llewellen Publications, 1998), xiii.

8. Ibid., xiv.

9. Anna Mulrine, "So You Want to Be a Teenage Witch?" *U.S. News & World Report,* March 1, 1999, 70.

10. Ellen G. White, *The Great Controversy* (Mountain View, CA: Pacific Press®, 1950), 624.

11. Ibid., 561.

CHAPTER 9

A Sign of the End:
The Growing Power
of the Papacy

Seventh-day Adventists have historically stated that a period of papal supremacy in Europe, which began in A.D. 538 and ended in 1798, dominated European politics as well as religion.* Of course, there was a period when the papacy *did* hold a powerful sway over the kings of Europe; however, the papacy didn't reach the pinnacle of this power until about the year 1200, and by the end of that century, a decline had already begun. So, it would be more accurate to say that the papacy's influence in secular affairs developed gradually over several centuries before 1200, and it declined gradually over several centuries after 1300.

The decline was largely due to two factors. The first was a revival of learning in Europe that began early in the second millennium with the establishment of universities—the University of Bologna in 1088, the University of Paris in 1150, Oxford in the early twelfth century, Cambridge in 1209, and so forth. Johannes Gutenberg's invention of the printing press in the mid-1400s gave a powerful boost to this increase in learning.

As people gain knowledge, they begin to challenge authority, and religion is one of the authorities that people especially tend to challenge. In Europe, this meant primarily the authority of the Roman Catholic Church.

---

* I devoted several chapters of my book *Could It* Really *Happen?* to an examination of the political ups and downs of the Roman Catholic Church during the past fifteen hundred years. This chapter is a summary of that material.

The increase of scientific knowledge proved especially detrimental to church authority. The church's authorities had adopted the position that the earth was stationary and the sun moved around it. They based this conclusion on 1 Chronicles 16:30, which says, "The world is firmly established; it cannot be moved." (See also Psalm 93:1; 96:10.) However, an astronomer by the name of Nicolaus Copernicus (1473–1543) concluded from his study of the heavens that the earth and the other planets circled the sun rather than the other way around. Galileo Galilei (1564–1642), one of the world's most famous early scientists, concluded that Copernicus was right. Upset with his views, the church put him on trial and coerced him into saying that the earth is stationary. (Legend has it, though, that after the trial he muttered, "And yet it moves!")[1] Eventually, of course, it became clear that Copernicus and Galileo were right and the church was wrong. This evidence of the church's fallibility began to undermine its credibility, and, ultimately, its authority.

The Protestant Reformation and the Enlightenment

The second factor in the decline of the power of the Roman Catholic Church was the Protestant Reformation. Prior to Martin Luther's time, the church had usually been successful in putting down challenges to its authority. During the 1300s, John Wycliffe, one of the earliest Reformers, got away with his criticism of the church. The popes opposed him bitterly but were unable to silence him. However, other Reformers weren't so fortunate. Two of the best known are John Huss and Jerome of Prague, both of whom were martyred for their faith. The Waldenses were also a special focus of the church's attack, and the Inquisition was responsible for the deaths of thousands of so-called heretics who opposed the teachings and authority of the papacy.

One of the primary reasons why the papacy was successful in putting down what it considered to be heresy was the fact that secular rulers supported the church by prosecuting dissenters. At the pope's request, kings and princes would turn over so-called heretics to the church for trial in ecclesiastical courts, and these political authorities would imprison and torture or execute those whom the ecclesiastical courts condemned.

However, by the sixteenth century, the political power of the papacy had waned to the point that the political leaders in some parts of Europe were willing to ignore its orders. That was the case in Saxony, the part of Germany where Martin Luther lived. Pope Leo X demanded that Luther be sent to Rome for trial, but the electors (princes) of Saxony demurred, and the Reformation spread rapidly throughout Europe. This was a powerful blow to the authority of the church.

Unfortunately, Luther in Germany, Calvin in France and Switzerland, and the Anglican Church in England adopted the same view of the relationship of church and state as the Roman Catholic Church held. Luther used the power of the state to persecute those he disagreed with; Calvin established a rigid church-state government in Geneva; and the Church of England used the arm of the state to prosecute the Puritans.

The eighteenth century saw the rise of the Enlightenment, a philosophy in which reason is considered the primary source of authority. This obviously contradicts the Christian view that Scripture is the final authority for religious and spiritual belief. Among those who led out in, or were influenced by, this movement during the eighteenth century were such famous people as Voltaire, Immanuel Kant, Thomas Jefferson, and Benjamin Franklin. The idea that reason should be the primary source of authority is alive and well today in the thinking of secular humanists.

While as Bible-believing Christians we hold to a higher authority than reason, we recognize that the Enlightenment had a profound and very positive effect in that it produced democratic governments that broke the Roman Catholic and Protestant churches' control of European governments. We see the most outstanding example of this changed understanding of the relationship between politics and religion in the American experiment in democracy. That's why America's Constitution requires the separation of church and state. The success of the American experiment has influenced many of the nations of Europe to adopt this principle.

The end of Rome's political domination of European politics

A more radical example of this revolt against the churches' domination of politics is the French Revolution, which began a little more than ten years after the American Revolution and continued through most of the 1790s. For hundreds of years, an absolute monarchy had ruled France and cooperated with the papacy. In 1789, within three years of the start of the French Revolution, that monarchy collapsed. Prior to the revolution, the Catholic Church owned about 10 percent of the land in France, much more than any other landowner in the nation. And though the church was exempt from government taxes, it imposed a 10 percent tax on people's income. Understandably, many people resented the power and wealth of the church. Following the fall of the monarchy, the state confiscated the property the church had owned. It also required Catholic clergy to take an oath of loyalty to the state rather than to the church. Many of the priests who refused to do so were hunted down and either deported or executed. Thousands of them died.

During the 1790s, the French general Napoleon Bonaparte set out to conquer Europe, and he was quite successful—for the next couple of decades France ruled much of Europe. Napoleon's victories included a large tract of land in central Italy called the Papal States, which had been part of the Catholic Church's holdings for more than a thousand years. Pius VI, the reigning pope, was powerless to protect this region from the French army. On February 10, 1798, the French general Berthier marched into Rome and demanded that Pius renounce his political authority over the Papal States. When the pope refused, Berthier took him prisoner and brought him to Valence in eastern France, where he died six weeks later. Thus, the year 1798 saw the political power that the Roman Catholic Church had wielded over European governments for hundreds of years receive an all but fatal blow.

Now here's a very significant point: about fifty years later, in the mid-nineteenth century, the tiny movement that was to become the Seventh-day Adventist Church began proclaiming that before the end of time, the Roman Catholic Church would regain its political domination of Europe *and extend it over the whole world*! At the time, this seemed like nonsense. Rome had lost the last vestiges of its power over European politics a mere fifty years earlier—and these people were saying that the papacy was supposed to gain political dominance of the whole world?

Nevertheless, Adventists preached it because Revelation 13 predicted it.

A brief review of Revelation 13:1–10 is in order at this point. We need to begin with Daniel 7:25.*

Daniel 7 and Revelation 13

In his vision of chapter 7, Daniel saw four great beasts arise from the sea. His angel interpreter told him they represented four great kingdoms that would arise. The first of these was Babylon, in which Daniel himself was living at the time. After Babylon came Media-Persia, Greece, and Rome. The beast symbolizing Rome had ten horns on its head, representing the nations of Europe that arose after the breakup of the fourth kingdom, the Roman Empire. Then another horn, a "little" one, grew up among these ten. This little horn was a powerful religio-political entity that blasphemed God, persecuted His people, and attacked His laws. The angel told Daniel that this horn would have a life span of "a time, times and half a time" (Daniel 7:25). The Aramaic word for time also means year (see Daniel 4:16, margin), so "a time, times and half a time" is three and a half years, or 1,260 days—based on a 360-day-long year. (See also Revelation 12:6, 14.) Applying the year-day principle, we arrive at 1,260 years. Most Adventist interpreters believe that this period began in A.D. 538 and ended in 1798—the year Pius VI was taken prisoner and the papacy lost its political power.

The powerful sea beast of Revelation 13:1–10 parallels the unnamed beast of Daniel 7:25 in its blasphemy and persecution, and, significantly, in its life span of forty-two months. Forty-two months of thirty days each equals 1,260 days—by now a familiar time period. The repetition of these symbols leaves no doubt that like Daniel 7's little horn, Revelation 13's beast from the sea represents the papacy. Note that Revelation 13 does have a significant detail that we don't find in Daniel 7—verse 3 says the beast from the sea received a "fatal wound."†

---

* For a more complete explanation of Daniel 7:25 and Revelation 13, see chapter 3 of my book *Could It* Really *Happen?*

† This is the New International Version's wording; the King James Version says "deadly wound," which has been the traditional term in Adventism.

There is another significant difference between Daniel 7's little horn and Revelation 13's beast from the sea. Whereas the little horn represents the papacy during the medieval period, the sea beast represents the papacy during the end time. And notice what verse 7 of Revelation 13 says about the sea beast: "It was given authority over every tribe, people, language and nation." It's on this basis that Adventists stated as early as the 1850s that the papacy's deadly wound would be healed—by which we meant that the papacy would gain global political power shortly before the second coming of Christ. Revelation 17:12, 13 is even more specific. It says that the nations of the earth will turn over their power and authority to this beast. As I said earlier, back in the 1850s this seemed to be nonsense. The papacy was losing, not gaining, influence and power. But, as I also pointed out, Adventists spoke of a resurgence of the papacy because Revelation predicted it—and developments during the past couple of hundred years have confirmed the accuracy of our interpretation.

The papacy since 1798

Napoleon returned control of the Papal States to the Vatican in 1800, but in 1870, during the Italian war of independence, Italy annexed the Papal States; and they have been under the control of the secular Italian government ever since.* Angry with the Italian government, for the next fifty years the popes imposed upon themselves a voluntary imprisonment inside the walls of the Vatican. However, this political isolation was destined to change. I will share three examples with you of the growing political power of the papacy in today's world.

The Lateran Treaty. In the early 1920s, Benito Mussolini became dictator of Italy. By this time both the Italian government and the papacy were ready for reconciliation, and, in 1929, they signed the Lateran Treaty, which gave the papacy full political control over 108 acres within the city of Rome. The Catholic Church once again became a nation, albeit with the smallest territory of any nation in the world. In the years

---

* It's reasonable to say, then, that while Napoleon defeated the papacy and thus fulfilled the specifications of the 1,260-year time period of Daniel 7:25, papal political power ebbed to its lowest point in 1870.

since that time, the Vatican has exchanged ambassadors with a majority of the world's nations and has become a powerful voice in world affairs.

At the time of the signing of the Lateran Treaty, some Seventh-day Adventists enthusiastically proclaimed that the deadly wound had been healed. In retrospect, that conclusion, while understandable, is quite inaccurate. It would be more correct to say that the signing of that treaty was the first step in the healing of the deadly wound. That process is still ongoing.

The Vatican and Hitler. Eugenio Pacelli was the Vatican's ambassador to Germany in the late 1920s. One of his ambitions was to sign a treaty with Germany like the one the Vatican signed with Italy. In February 1930, Pope Pius XI made Pacelli the Vatican's secretary of state. Three years later, Hitler became chancellor of Germany. He, too, wanted to have a treaty with the Vatican—but there was a problem: Germany was about two-thirds Protestant and one-third Catholic, so the German *Reichstag* (congress) wasn't interested in such a treaty.

However, Hitler came up with a scheme to override that opposition. A clause in the German constitution provided that, in a national emergency, the chancellor could be given dictatorial powers by a two-thirds vote of the Reichstag. Hitler's Nazi Party didn't have the necessary two-thirds. However, the Vatican, which was also anxious to conclude a treaty with Germany, persuaded the German Catholic party—called the Center Party—to side with Hitler's Nazi Party, and this coalition was enough to give Hitler the two-thirds majority in the Reichstag that he needed to assume dictatorial powers. The Nazi Party and the Center Party cast their votes, and a few weeks later Hitler signed his treaty with the Vatican. This is another example of the papacy's growing political influence in the world.

The Vatican and the fall of Communism. The Polish cardinal Karol Józef Wojtyła became Pope John Paul II in 1978. A couple of years later, Ronald Reagan was sworn in as the fortieth president of the United States, and a year and a half after that, on June 7, 1982, Pope John Paul II and President Reagan met alone in the Vatican library for forty-five minutes, during which time they reached a critical agreement: they would unite their forces in an effort to end Communism in Poland with the hope that this would free all of Eastern Europe from Communist domination. The story of their success is fascinating.

In the autumn of 1980, the Solidarity labor union organized a strike at Poland's shipyards in the port city of Gdansk. At first the government permitted the union to exist, but as unrest spread throughout Poland, the prime minister, Wojciech Jaruzelski, declared martial law and outlawed the union. John Paul's part of the bargain with Reagan was to provide moral support to the Polish people and the Solidarity union. The pope took three trips to his homeland in the early 1980s, and, on these trips, he encouraged his fellow citizens and the nation's Catholic leaders to resist the Communist government but to avoid pushing them too far too fast. He also gave permission for chapters of the Solidarity union to meet secretly in Catholic churches.

Reagan provided the Polish resistance with money and technology, sending computers, fax machines, printers, and other equipment to Denmark, where it was unloaded from United States containers and transferred to containers that didn't identify the country of origin. These containers were then transported to Poland's Gdansk shipyard, where loyal members of Solidarity surreptitiously distributed the contraband to Solidarity groups in Catholic churches around the country.

By early 1989, Solidarity's resistance to the Communist government of Poland had grown so strong that Jaruzelski appealed to Moscow for military assistance to crush the rebellion. However, Mikhail Gorbachev refused to send in the troops, and in June, the Communist government was forced to permit parliamentary elections. By the end of the year, Jaruzelski was out and Lech Walesa, the leader of Solidarity, was elected president of Poland.

The resistance to Soviet domination spread. The Berlin Wall, which divided free West Berlin from Communist East Berlin, was torn down in late November 1989. By early 1990, all the nations of Eastern Europe had broken away from Communist domination. And in December 1991, it was Gorbachev out, Yeltsin in, bringing the end to the Soviet Union. Communism was finished as a political force in Europe.*

---

* Several Communist parties are still active in European nations, including Russia, but they have no significant political influence.

A sign of the end

The point of all this is that during the twentieth century, the Roman Catholic Church became a major player in world politics once again. By early 2010, the Vatican had established diplomatic relations with nearly all of the 191 countries that are widely recognized as sovereign states.[2] John Paul II was an extremely popular pope during his twenty-seven-year pontificate. He was the most-traveled pope in Catholic history—traveling more than all the other popes combined. Billy Graham called him "the moral conscience of the whole Christian world,"[3] and *Christianity Today* ran a series of articles about him, including one titled "He Was My Pope Too."[4] His funeral was attended by what was—other than some meetings of the United Nations—the largest gathering of heads of state in history. Among the mourners were four kings, five queens, and seventy presidents and prime ministers. An estimated four million other mourners gathered in Rome—probably the single largest gathering in Christian history—and it's estimated that more than two billion people watched the funeral on television.[5] Twenty-three Orthodox and eight Protestant delegations were present, and former United States presidents George H. W. Bush and Bill Clinton knelt for five minutes in front of John Paul's casket.

According to Revelation 13, one of the final developments prior to Christ's second coming was to be the restoration of the global political power of the papacy—what Revelation calls the healing of the sea beast's fatal wound. It's evident that during the twentieth century, major strides were taken toward fulfilling that specification. We can view the resurgence of papal political power as a highly significant indication that the world is approaching the end of human history as we know it.

The delay in Christ's return is nearing its end.

---

1. http://en.wikipedia.org/wiki/Galileo_Galilei. Actually, there is no evidence that he said this.

2. http://en.wikipedia.org/wiki/List_of_sovereign_states.

3. David van Biema, "Pope John Paul II, 1920–2005: A Defender of the Faith," *Time*, April 11, 2005, 36, http://www.time.com/time/magazine/article/0,9171,1044716,00.html.

4. http://www.christianitytoday.com/ct/2005/aprilweb-only/16.0.html.
5. http://en.wikipedia.org/wiki/Funeral_of_Pope_John_Paul_II.

CHAPTER 10

A Sign of the End: Church-State Separation Under Attack

There's a tug of war going on in America. The issue is the relationship that should exist between the church and the state. Religious Right enthusiasts would have the state become a Christian nation that enforces the moral principles of the church. Secularists want to rid government of every vestige of religion or support for religion.

In the previous chapter, I pointed out that the United States pioneered the principle of church-state separation, and most of the nations of the Western world have adopted some form of that principle. However, the study of Bible prophecy has convinced Seventh-day Adventists that this will end someday, and the United States government will persecute people because of their practice of religion. That's difficult to believe, given the religious pluralism that has existed in this country for almost 250 years. However, just as our prediction about the end-time renewal of the political power of the papacy is based on Bible prophecy, so is our prediction about persecution in America. In a very broad sense, we can understand Jesus Himself to have made this prediction. He told His disciples that shortly before His second coming, they "will be hated by all nations because of me" (Matthew 24:9). The United States is one of those nations, so it shouldn't surprise us to discover that Revelation 13 predicts that it will experience the rise of persecution.

The land beast of Revelation 13

Revelation 13 pictures two great beasts. The first, which we discussed in chapter 9, rises from the sea, and the second rises from the earth. Verse 11 says of the second beast that "he had two horns like a lamb, but he spoke like a dragon." Seventh-day Adventists believe that this beast represents the United States. I will briefly mention four reasons why we interpret the prophecy this way.

First, a beast in Bible prophecy generally represents a major political power—a nation (see Daniel 7 and 8).

Second, the land beast has global political authority; Revelation 13:12 says that it "made the earth and its inhabitants worship the first beast." (See also verse 14.)

Third, the land beast is an end-time nation—it enforces the mark of the beast, which is an end-time phenomenon (see verses 16, 17).

Finally, the land beast is a Christian nation—note that verse 11 says that this beast has the appearance of a lamb. The word *lamb* occurs thirty-one times in Revelation, and in every instance except this one it is a symbol of Jesus Christ. Here it represents a false christ, because it speaks like a dragon—that is, like Satan (see Revelation 12:9).

The United States fulfills each of these specifications, and no other nation does.

1. It is obviously a nation.
2. It is the only nation in today's world that has global political influence.
3. Earlier in this book we established that we today live in the end time, so we can say that the United States is an end-time nation.
4. And the United States has historically been a predominantly Christian nation.

Now let's examine three other details about this land beast. First, it's the enforcement arm of the papacy. This is evident from the fact that this beast sets up an image to the first beast (verse 14), and the image to the beast causes the whole world to worship the first beast, the papacy (verse

15). During the medieval period, secular governments were the enforcement arm of the papacy, and that's the function of the land beast.

Second, the land beast unites church and state. This is evident from the fact that the land beast, the United States, enforces papal teachings. This is exactly the same relationship that existed between secular governments and the church during the medieval period.

And third, the land beast is a persecuting power—it threatens the livelihood of those who defy its support of the beast from the sea (verses 16, 17), and it threatens to execute anyone who refuses to worship the sea beast (verse 15).

This brief overview of the land beast of Revelation 13 clearly indicates that the United States will someday abandon its historic commitment to church-state separation, for only in this way could the United States begin to persecute religious dissenters. So long as religion and government continue to operate in separate spheres, neither exercising undue influence over the other, America will be free of religious persecution. But when religion gains a dominant influence over politics, it's inevitable that dissenters will be persecuted. It may not happen immediately. Indeed, I expect that the promoters of church-state union will insist that they don't wish to oppress dissenters. But that *will* eventually happen. It's inevitable anytime religion gains a position that enables it to control society. I wouldn't want my own church, the Seventh-day Adventist Church, to gain that much influence over government, because I believe that in due time we also would succumb to the temptation to enforce our beliefs by law. No matter how innocuous a religion may be, whenever it gains that kind of influence, it excuses its persecution of dissenters by saying something to the effect that "we're just trying to establish moral order in society." *Always fear any religion that tries to enforce its moral agenda through the political process.*

The Protestant threat to church-state separation in America

Given the history of church-state separation and America's tolerance of all religions, it's hard to believe that such a state of affairs could develop in this country. However, as I said, we believe this will happen because Bible prophecy predicts it. So, we must ask whether there's any indication that the United States is moving in the direction of breaking down the wall of separation between church and state that has existed for the better part of 250 years. The answer is Yes, and we see that movement coming especially from the branch of American Protestantism popularly known as the Religious Right. Again, my explanation will involve a summary of several chapters from my book *Could It Really Happen?*[1]

I first became aware of this trend in the United States back in about 1987, when I read an article that quoted Pat Robertson's rants against the "evils" of church-state separation. Since then, this perspective has become increasingly popular among Religious Right Christians, both Protestant and Catholic. Today, millions of Americans have been led to believe that the founders of this country didn't really intend church and state to be kept separate. Please note the following quotes by influential American Protestants:

Pat Robertson: "They [liberals and secularists] have kept us in submission because they have talked about separation of church and state. There is no such thing in the Constitution. It's a lie of the left, and we're not going to take it anymore."[2]

"We have had a distortion imposed on us over the past few years by left-wingers who have fastened themselves into the court system. And we have had a lie foisted on us that there is something embedded in the Constitution called separation of church and state."[3]

"[The courts] are taking our religion away from us under the guise of separation of church and state."[4]

Jerry Falwell: "Separation of Church and State has long been the battle cry of civil libertarians wishing to purge our glorious Christian heritage from our nation's history. Of course, the term never once appears in our Constitution and is a modern fabrication of discrimination."[5]

W. A. Criswell, former senior pastor of the Dallas First Baptist Church: "There is no such thing as separation of church and state. It is merely a figment of the imagination of infidels."[6]

D. James Kennedy, former Presbyterian pastor in Fort Lauderdale, Florida: "If we are committed and involved in taking back the nation for Christian moral values, . . . there is no doubt we can witness the dismantling of not just the Berlin wall but the even more diabolical 'wall of separation' that has led to secularization, godlessness, immorality, and corruption in our country."[7]

Francis Schaeffer, prominent Christian philosopher of the mid-twentieth century: "Today the separation of church and state in America is used to silence the church."[8]

And religious leaders aren't the only ones supporting the attack on church-state separation. Note the following.

William Rehnquist, at the time associate justice of the United States Supreme Court. He served as chief justice of that court from 1986 to 2005: "The 'wall of separation between church and state' is a metaphor based on bad history, a metaphor which has proved useless as a guide to judging. It should be frankly and explicitly abandoned."[9]

Tom DeLay, former United States House majority leader, in a speech on the floor of the House of Representatives: "To claim that our Founding Fathers were for separation of church and state is either rewriting history or being very ignorant of history."[10]

Jay Alan Seculow, chief counsel for the American Center for Law and Justice: "I've had it with the ACLU's outrageous attacks on our nation's religious heritage and our right to express our faith publicly. . . . What's frustrating about this is that their entire argument is based on the utterly false principle of 'separation of church and state.' . . . There is no 'wall' of separation!

"The fact is, the phrase 'separation of church and state' is not found in the U.S. Constitution, the framework of our freedom. . . . Too often, the 'separation of church and state' phrase is allowed to take the place of our actual constitutional provisions."[11]

In a similar vein, the Web site TheocracyWatch calls attention to a speech that Antonin Scalia, associate justice of the United States Supreme Court, made on January 12, 2003, at a Religious Freedom Day event. In his speech, Scalia said the principle of church-state separation wasn't embedded in the Constitution and therefore should be added democratically, which means through a constitutional amendment. TheocracyWatch points out, correctly, that an amendment to the Constitution on church-state separation would be impossible to achieve in the current political climate, so the argument is pointless.[12]

It's true that the phrase "separation of church and state" doesn't appear in the American Constitution—but that's true also of several other principles that are foundational to our legal system—among them, "fair trial," "innocent until proven guilty," and the "right against self-incrimination."[13] However, even though the terms themselves aren't in the Constitution, the principles that these terms express *are* there. Likewise, while the words "separation of church and state" don't appear in the Constitution, the First Amendment says, "Congress shall make no law respecting an establishment of religion, or prohibiting the free exercise thereof." Clearly, this amendment separates religion and politics in the United States, and that's what church-state separation is all about.

The Catholic threat to church-state separation in America

In ancient times, religion and government were virtually inseparable. In the Roman Empire, the emperor was the official head of the state religion. Nobody back then had ever thought of keeping religion and government separate. Thus, it's not surprising that the Catholic Church, which evolved out of the Roman Empire, adopted the principle of church-state union at the beginning of its existence and has maintained that principle to the present time. And, of course, to the Catholic way of thinking, in the ideal state, Catholicism would be the national religion.

On June 20, 1888, Pope Leo XIII issued an encyclical, titled "On the Nature of Human Liberty." In this encyclical, he said that

> means and opportunities [must be provided] whereby the community may be enabled to live properly, that is to say, according to the laws of God. For, since God is the source of all goodness and justice, it is absolutely ridiculous that the State should pay no attention to these laws or render them abortive by contrary enactments.[14]

Of course, by "laws of God," Leo meant God's laws as Catholics understand them.

Pius IX said that one of the "principal errors of our time" is the idea that "the Church ought to be separate from the State and the State from the Church."[15] Leo XIII considered the idea of church-state separation to be "a fatal principle."[16] And the Catholic historian George La Piana said the Catholic Church condemns church-state separation "as an offense of God's law and a fatal source of evil."[17]

Some people may argue that this has all changed since the Vatican II ecumenical council,* and for those who want evidence, they point to the council's "Declaration on Religious Freedom," which states,

> This Vatican Council declares that the human person has a right to religious freedom. This freedom means that all men are to be immune from coercion on the part of individuals or of social groups and of any human power, in such wise that no one is to be forced to act in a manner contrary to his own beliefs, whether privately or publicly, whether alone or in association with others, within due limits.[18]

---

* Vatican Council II was the twenty-first ecumenical council of the Catholic Church. It was conducted in four sessions from October 11, 1962, to December 8, 1965.

We must keep two points in mind as we evaluate this statement. First, while related, religious liberty and church-state separation aren't the same thing. Liberty of conscience means what the Vatican II declaration stated: that no one should be forced to act contrary to his or her religious beliefs—or, to put it another way, all people should be free to practice their religion without coercion so long as their practice doesn't infringe on the rights of other people. Church-state separation, on the other hand, means that the church and the state will operate in separate spheres, neither having too much influence on the other. Church-state separation provides the ideal context for the nurture of religious freedom.

The second thing to keep in mind in evaluating the Vatican council's positive statement on religious freedom is that the Catholic Church has never diverged from its support of church-state union. To the Catholic mind, in the ideal state, the government will enforce the moral principles of the church, that is, of the Catholic Church.

A prime example of this is the Catholic insistence on overturning the United States Supreme Court's 1973 decision in *Roe v. Wade,* which legalized abortion. Most Adventists probably agree that abortion on demand is wrong, and the case can certainly be made that the unborn deserve the protection of the government as much as do those who have been born. However, if the Catholic Church were to become the religion of the state, all forms of contraception would be banned, including surgical sterilization. That ban would include artificial insemination, in vitro fertilization, and all other forms of assisted reproductive technologies. There is no doubt that in a Catholic-dominated government, legislation would also set Sunday aside as a national day of rest,* and numerous other moral principles of the Roman Catholic Church would also become the law of the land. And over time, this breakdown in the principle of church-state separation would inevitably lead to prosecution of dissenters.

One hundred years ago, Ellen White wrote, "Let the principle once be established in the United States that the church may employ or control the power of the state; that religious observances may be enforced by

---

* For more information about Sunday laws, see chapter 14 of this book.

secular laws; in short, that the authority of church and state is to domi-nate the conscience, and the triumph of Rome in this country is as-sured."[19] Today's Roman Catholic Church is not advocating the aboli-tion of church-state separation in America as vigorously as Religious Right Protestants are, but you can be certain that they would willingly accept this change were it to occur. When it happens—and Revelation 13 says it will—Catholics will surely give it their full support.

Recent political trends in the United States

In 1979, Jerry Falwell established an organization called the Moral Majority. Throughout the 1980s, the Moral Majority tried very hard to get Religious Right candidates elected to national office. But Falwell overlooked one reality: national leaders are elected at the grassroots level. To have a significant effect on national politics, one must start at the lo-cal level.

Falwell's Moral Majority died in 1989, which led secular pundits to declare the Religious Right to be dead. They were startled out of their complacency by Pat Robertson's Christian Coalition, which, under the leadership of Ralph Reed, focused strongly on organizing political sup-port at the local level. The 1994 midterm election took the control of the United States Congress from the Democrats, who had held it for some sixty years, and gave it to the Republicans. In fact, the Democrats lost eight seats in the Senate, giving the Republicans a four-seat majority, and they lost fifty-four seats in the House of Representatives, giving the Re-publicans a twenty-six-seat majority! The Republicans held control of both houses of Congress for the next twelve years.

Time magazine featured Ralph Reed on the cover of its May 15, 1995, issue. The caption beside a black-and-white picture of Reed said, "The Right Hand of God: Meet Ralph Reed, 33. His Christian Coalition is on a crusade to take over U.S. politics—and it's working."[20] The Religious Right had resurrected! The article on the inside described the Christian Coalition as "formidable" and "one of the most powerful grassroots or-ganizations in American politics."[21]

In 2000, George W. Bush, who is conservative both politically and religiously, was strongly favored by the Religious Right. However, he actually won fewer popular votes than his opponent, Al Gore—50,456,002 votes for Bush to 50,999,897 for Gore.[22] The question of which of the two won the Florida electoral votes ended up in the Supreme Court, which ruled that Bush was the winner. As president, Bush supported a number of Religious Right issues, among them, adding a marriage amendment to the United States Constitution, supporting teacher-led prayer in public schools and vouchers for public school students, and placing restrictions on abortion.

By the time of the 2004 election, the war in Iraq was going badly, and it's probably correct to say that the majority of Americans expected his Democratic opponent, John Kerry, to win. However, Bush ended up the victor. No doubt the tide was turned in Bush's favor by a number of factors. I suspect that two religious matters strongly influenced the outcome. First, John Kerry was a Catholic, but he supported freedom of choice regarding abortion, which likely caused him to lose the majority of the Catholic vote. Second, during the year prior to the election, the Massachusetts Supreme Court ruled for the first time in American history that homosexuals had a right to marry, and Gavin Newsom, the mayor of San Francisco, ordered the city clerk to issue marriage licenses to homosexuals.

The 2008 election was a huge disaster for the Religious Right and the conservative political movement. Barack Obama, a liberal Democrat, was elected president by a landslide, and the Democrats, who already controlled both houses of Congress, picked up eight more seats in the Senate and twenty-one more seats in the House of Representatives. Again, the pundits proclaimed the demise of the conservative political movement and the Religious Right.

Then came the Tea Party. While it's a political movement, people who would be classified as belonging to the Religious Right make up a significant part of the membership. On October 5, 2010, the *Washington Post* reported that a poll showed that "half of those who consider themselves part of the tea party movement also identify as part of the religious right."[23] And "fifty-five percent of people who say they are part of the tea party agree that 'America has always been and is currently a Christian nation'—6 points more than the percentage of self-described Christian conservatives who would say that."[24]

The liberal media and its commentators tend to dismiss the Religious Right as something just short of the lunatic fringe in American politics, and they are glad to begin writing epitaphs for the movement's gravestone whenever there's a significant reversal of the Religious Right's political interests. However, my observation over the past several years is that conservative politicians and their Religious Right bedfellows quite consistently tend to have resurrections.

It's not difficult to imagine that a major national or global crisis could push a significant portion of the population toward the Religious Right, making that group the dominant force in American politics. I believe that if Religious Right Protestants and Roman Catholics ever become serious about joining their forces, they could elect just about any candidate and enact just about any law they want to. The fact that they largely agree in their views on church-state separation is sobering to contemplate.

A sign of the end

In his introduction to Dudley Canright's book *Seventh-day Adventism Renounced,* Theodore Nelson wrote, "The rejection by the United States of its historic support of religious freedom would require a greater miracle than for God to grow a giant oak in an instant."[25] I can understand Nelson's saying that in the context of the United States in 1889, when Canright's book was first published. Even today, a casual glance at the current state of American politics would hardly presage imminent persecution for religious beliefs. However, if the foundation of religious freedom lies in keeping church and state separate, then the evidence that I have presented in this chapter suggests that religious freedom in the United States could quickly disappear if the Religious Right were to gain control of the government.

Jesus' prediction that those who follow Him "will be hated by all nations" (Matthew 24:9) suggests that before the end of time, every country in the world will persecute His people. And John's description of the second beast of Revelation 13 makes it clear that the United States *will* become a persecuting power, one that enforces the doctrinal precepts of the Roman Catholic Church. Prophecy clearly predicts this, and current events in the United States make this prospect more believable now than it has been at any previous time in the nation's history.

This, to me, is another indication that *the delay in Christ's return is nearing its end.*

---

1. Marvin Moore, *Could It Really Happen?* (Nampa, ID: Pacific Press®, 2007).

2. From a November 1993 address by Pat Robertson, cited in Anti-Defamation League, *The Religious Right: The Assault on Tolerance and Pluralism in America* (New York: Anti-Defamation League, 1994), 4.

3. Pat Robertson, on October 12, 2002, at the Christian Coalition's "Road to Victory" conference, cited on the Web site of Americans United for Separation of Church and State, "Christian Broadcasting Network," http://www.au.org/resources/religious -right-research/organizations/christian-broadcasting.html.

4. Pat Robertson, on his television program *The 700 Club,* July 19, 2005, cited in Rob Boston in "Religious Right Power Brokers: The Top Ten," *Church and State,* June 2006, 14.

5. Jerry Falwell, cited in Rob Boston, "Religious Right Power Brokers: The Top Ten," *Church and State,* June 2006, 14.

6. From a CBS interview of September 6, 1984, taped the day after he delivered the benediction at the Republican National Convention, cited in Anti-Defamation League, 4.

7. Cited in Rob Boston, "D. James Kennedy: Who Is He and What Does He Want?" Americans United for Separation of Church and State, http://www.au.org /media/church-and-state/archives/1999/04/d-james-kennedy.html.

8. Francis A Schaeffer, *A Christian Manifesto* (Westchester, IL: Crossway Books, 1981), 36.

9. Wallace v. Jaffree, 472 U.S. 38 (1984).

10. Cited in *Signswatch,* Winter 2001, 3.

11. Cited in Rob Boston, "Religious Right Power Brokers: The Top Ten," 13.

12. "Biblical Law," The Rise of the Religious Right in the Republican Party, http:// www.theocracywatch.org/biblical_law2.htm.

13. For a long list of these terms, see Leonard W. Levy, *Original Intent and the Framers' Constitution* (Chicago: Ivan R. Dee, 1988), 351.

14. Leo XIII, "On the Nature of Human Liberty," par. 18, http://www.papalencyclicals .net/Leo13/l13liber.htm.

15. Pius IX, "Syllabus of Errors," no. 55, http://www.papalencyclicals.net/Pius09 /p9syll.htm.

16. Leo XIII, par. 38.

17. George La Piana and John Swomley, *Catholic Power vs. American Freedom* (Amherst, NY: Prometheus Books, 2002), 20.

18. Vatican II, "Declaration on Religious Freedom," no. 2, http://www.vatican.va /archive/hist_councils/ii_vatican_council/documents/vat-ii_decl_19651207_dignitatis -humanae_en.html.

19. White, *The Great Controversy*, 581.

20. *Time,* May 15, 1995, cover.

21. Jeffrey H. Birnbaum, "The Gospel According to Ralph Reed," *Time,* May 15, 1995, 28, 30.

22. Federal Election Commission, "2000 Presidential Popular Vote Summary for All Candidates Listed on at Least One State Ballot," http://www.fec.gov/pubrec /fe2000/prespop.htm.

23. Michelle Boorstein, "Tea Party, Religious Right Often Overlap, Poll Shows," *Washington Post,* October 5, 2010, http://www.washingtonpost.com/wp-dyn/content /article/2010/10/05/AR2010100501491.html.

24. Ibid.

25. Theodore Nelson, introduction to *Seventh-day Adventism Renounced,* by Dudley M. Canright (Nashville: Gospel Advocate Company, 1914), 23.

CHAPTER 11

A Sign of the End: Religious Persecution in America

Adventists have been quite severely scorned over the years for our belief that the United States of America will become a persecuting power during the final years of earth's history. A case in point is what the former Seventh-day Adventist minister Dudley Canright said in his book *Seventh-day Adventism Renounced:* "Of all the wild Advent speculations in the prophecies, this deserves to stand among the wildest."[1] And in the introduction to Canright's book, Theodore Nelson wrote, "This ostentatious martyr-spirit of our Adventist friends seems quite absurd."[2]

We can understand people thinking so. After all, the First Amendment to the American Constitution says, "Congress shall make no law respecting an establishment of religion, or prohibiting the free exercise thereof." In order for the United States to persecute religious dissenters, a change will have to take place, if not in the Constitution itself, at least in its interpretation.

And Ellen White predicted just such a change. She wrote,

> When Protestantism shall stretch her hand across the gulf to grasp the hand of the Roman power, when she shall reach over the abyss to clasp hands with spiritualism, when, under the influence of this three-fold union, our country shall repudiate every principle of its Constitution as a Protestant and republican gov-

ernment, . . . then we may know that the time has come for the marvelous working of Satan and that the end is near.[3]

So who's right, Dudley Canright and Theodore Nelson or Ellen White? American history and current events both suggest that persecution could indeed arise in this nation.

History

Many people don't realize that American history includes a significant number of incidents in which a religious minority was persecuted by the religious majority. The Puritans, for instance, were quite severely persecuted in sixteenth-century England for their beliefs and practices. Eventually, some of them ventured out on the long and dangerous journey across the Atlantic Ocean in a small sailing vessel. They hoped to have in America the religious freedom the authorities in their homeland withheld.

Unfortunately, when they arrived, they set up their own theocracy and denied others what they had been so intent on obtaining for themselves. They passed strict Sunday laws that forbade so much as a husband and wife kissing in public;[4] they banned Roger Williams from Salem, Massachusetts, for his liberal views on freedom of religion; they hanged several Quakers because they refused to give up their faith; they executed nineteen people because they presumed them to be witches; and, in the decade before the American Revolution, they fined people professing to be Baptists, whipped them, and locked them in jail for "crimes" related to their faith.[5]

The Puritan persecutions mentioned in the paragraph above took place before the founding of America as a nation, but people have suffered religious persecution in this country since its founding too. During the 1800s, immigrants from the Catholic countries of Europe flooded the United States. The memory of persecutions carried out by Catholics in Europe was still fresh in the minds of Protestant Americans, and many of them feared that the Catholic immigrants would try to establish the authority of their church in America. As a result, a strong anti-Catholic, "nativist" movement developed. This movement was responsible for fierce anti-Catholic riots.

The first such riots took place in Philadelphia in May and July 1844.[6] A decade later, an anti-Catholic riot in Louisville, Kentucky, resulted in more than a hundred businesses and homes being vandalized and Catholic citizens being attacked on the streets and in their homes. Conservative estimates put the death toll at twenty-two.[7] And on July 12, 1871, 150 people were wounded and more than sixty people, mostly Catholics, were killed in a riot between Catholics and Protestants in New York City.[8]

And in the late 1880s and early 1890s, in Arkansas, Tennessee, and Georgia, several Seventh-day Adventists experienced religious persecution. They were jailed and fined for violating Sunday laws. Thus, it's evident that while America has largely been a land of religious freedom, sporadic popular sentiment against particular religious groups has resulted in limited but significant persecution.

Current events

Could the same thing happen in America again? I think it's already happening in a minor way, and recent events indicate that a more intense persecution could develop.

It seems to me that there are two factors that can lead to persecution: fear, and religious differences between members of a population. During the Inquisition of the Middle Ages, persecution arose primarily because the authorities in the established church disagreed vehemently with the doctrinal views held by the minority. But the persecution of Catholics in America during the 1800s wasn't driven so much by the doctrinal differences between Catholics and Protestants as it was by a profound fear that as the number of Catholics increased, they would take over the country.

Adventists have generally considered that it is the doctrinal differences between them and major religious groups—especially regarding the Sabbath—that will stir up persecution during the final crisis. While that will surely be one factor in producing the trouble, I believe the persecution of the last days will be driven especially by fear.

This is particularly evident in the attitudes of Americans toward Muslims since the terrorist attacks on the Pentagon and New York City's Twin Towers. Following those attacks, hate crimes against people of Middle Eastern descent increased from 354 attacks in 2000 to 1,501 in 2001,[9] and most of the increase occurred in the last four months of 2001.

A number of incidents in the years since 9/11 illustrate the role that fear can play in the persecution of a minority—in this case, Muslims. You've no doubt heard about the proposal to build an Islamic center two blocks from the site where the two towers of the World Trade Center used to stand. A storm of protest erupted following the announcement of the construction plans, though the opposition was primarily about the proximity of the Islamic center to the World Trade Center and not to the idea of Muslims building a mosque in New York City.

In other parts of the country, the opposition was more directly against Muslims and their religion. For instance, hundreds of protestors objected when Muslims in Murfreesboro, Tennessee, obtained a building permit to construct a mosque just outside the city. The protestors feared that the facility would be turned into a training center for terrorists. Some people vandalized the sign that depicted the future Islamic center, and several hundred demonstrators wore T-shirts that said, "Vote for Jesus" and carried placards that said, "No sharia law for USA." One man protested, "They aren't a religion. They're a political, militaristic group," and another said, "No mosque in Murfreesboro. I don't want them here. Go start their own country overseas somewhere. This is a Christian country. It's based on Christianity." A candidate for Congress accused the center of fostering terrorism and trying to establish ties to the militant Palestinian group Hamas. And on August 28, 2010, someone poured gasoline on some construction equipment at the site and set it on fire. There were also reports of guns being fired near the mosque site.[10]

On Election Day 2010, nearly 70 percent of the citizens of Oklahoma voted in favor of a ballot measure that blocks judges from considering sharia law and international law when deciding cases. Christian conservatives there insist that they had to ban the courts from using sharia law in order to thwart what they believed was an effort by radical Muslims to impose that law in the United States.

On November 25, 2010, Vicki Miles-LaGrange, a federal judge, temporarily blocked Oklahoma from putting the new law into effect. She said the law discriminates against one religion, thus favoring other religions, and, therefore, it was a violation of the First Amendment to the American Constitution, which forbids the government from becoming involved in religious affairs.[11]

The fear that sharia law might influence the decisions of some American judges has some basis in reality. Great Britain has given sharia judges authority to rule on certain financial disputes and domestic cases, including divorce, and these rulings are subject to enforcement by the nation's judicial system.[12] In 1991, to help the courts deal with a large backlog of cases, the province of Ontario in Canada approved the use of faith-based tribunals to make decisions in Catholic and Jewish disputes over divorce, inheritance, and child custody. Nobody seemed to mind that, but there was a huge outcry when the Islamic Institute of Civil Justice announced that it intended to establish similar tribunals throughout the province so they could settle domestic disputes according to sharia law.[13]

Then there's the famous case of the Dove World Outreach Center—a small, nondenominational church in Gainesville, Florida. Terry Jones, the pastor of this church, announced plans to burn thousands of copies of the Koran on September 11, 2010, the ninth anniversary of the 9/11 attacks. He also encouraged people around the world to burn Korans on that day, which he called "Burn a Koran Day." Jones said, "We believe that Islam is of the devil, that it's causing billions of people to go to hell. It is a deceptive religion, it is a violent religion, and that has been proven many, many times."[14]

This is a small sampling of the bigotry and persecution against Muslims that has developed in the United States since 9/11. I propose that the driving force behind this persecution is a fear that the religio-political ideology of Muslims in the Middle East, especially their sharia law, might replace the principles of religious and political freedom on which the American government is based.

Is it relevant?

Does the fact that Catholics and Muslims have suffered persecution in America justify the belief that some time in the future some American Christians will persecute other American Christians? After all, the incidents of persecution of Catholics happened more than a hundred years ago, and, for all practical purposes, prejudice against Catholics ended with the election of John F. Kennedy as president in 1960.

The significance of the persecution of Catholics and Muslims in America lies not so much in the incidents themselves as in what motivated them. During the 1800s, it was the fear that Catholic immigrants would eventually try to force their religion on the whole nation. And the Americans who have attacked Muslims and their institutions since 9/11 have been motivated by a profound fear of a Muslim takeover in the United States. Commenting on the mosque controversy in Murfreesboro, Tennessee, former county commissioner Jim Daniel said, "What I sense is a certain amount of fear fueling the animosity, [a fear that] the Muslims coming in here will keep growing in numbers and override our system of law and impose sharia law."[15]

It seems that fear will launch the unprecedented persecution prophesied in Scripture and by Ellen White—fear generated by societal disruptions perhaps caused in part by conflict with people who differ in their religion and in other ways, but even more by what will be happening in the physical world at that time. Both Scripture and Ellen White associate terrible natural disasters with the final crisis.[16] I propose that the threat posed by these natural disasters will spark a deep fear, which will in turn generate an intense anger against Sabbath keepers. This anger, then, will play out in persecution of the people belonging to this minority religion. Ellen White wrote,

> The great deceiver will persuade men that those who serve God are causing these evils [natural disasters]. The class that have provoked the displeasure of Heaven will charge all their troubles upon those whose obedience to God's commandments is a perpetual reproof to transgressors. It will be declared that men are

offending God by the violation of the Sunday sabbath; that this sin has brought calamities which will not cease until Sunday observance shall be strictly enforced; and that those who present the claims of the fourth commandment, thus destroying reverence for Sunday, are troublers of the people, preventing their restoration to divine favor and temporal prosperity. . . . As the wrath of the people shall be excited by false charges, they will pursue a course toward God's ambassadors very similar to that which apostate Israel pursued toward Elijah.[17]

Satan puts his interpretation upon events, and the [people] think, as he would have them, that the calamities which fill the land are a result of Sundaybreaking. Thinking to appease the wrath of God, these influential men make laws enforcing Sunday observance.[18]

A sign of the end

So, is religious persecution possible in America? At the present time, no—at least not the kind of persecution that Scripture and Ellen White predict. However, as I pointed out in the previous chapter, Jesus warned that before the end of time, those who follow Him "will be hated by all nations" (Matthew 24:9). The United States is a nation, and this alone is enough to indicate that persecution will happen in this country. If the Adventist interpretation of the second beast of Revelation 13 is correct—which I believe it is—then at some point in the future this nation will become responsible for horrible persecutions based on people's beliefs about religion.

There is always a danger of assuming that the present condition of society will extend indefinitely into the future. Time after time this assumption has proved to be false. The attacks on Catholics during the 1800s and the recent attacks on Muslim people and Islamic institutions in the United States, while relatively minor, are clear indications that, given the right circumstances, Americans are fully capable of persecuting dissenters.

This, to me, is another indication that *the delay in Christ's return is nearing its end.*

1. Canright, 89.

2. Theodore Nelson, introduction to Canright, 23.

3. White, *Testimonies for the Church,* 5:451.

4. See Moore, *Could It* Really *Happen?* 102.

5. See ibid., 102–107.

6. http://en.wikipedia.org/wiki/Philadelphia_Nativist_Riot.

7. http://en.wikipedia.org/wiki/Bloody_Monday.

8. http://en.wikipedia.org/wiki/Orange_riots.

9. http://en.wikipedia.org/wiki/Persecution_of_muslims#United_States.

10. "Fire at Tenn. Mosque Building Site Ruled Arson," *CBS News,* August 30, 2010, http://www.cbsnews.com/stories/2010/08/28/national/main6814690.shtml.

11. James J. McKinley Jr., "Judge Blocks Oklahoma's Ban on Using Shariah Law in Court," *New York Times,* November 29, 2010, http://www.nytimes.com/2010/11/30/us/30oklahoma.html.

12. Abul Taher, "Revealed: UK's First Official Sharia Courts," *Sunday Times,* September 14, 2008; http://www.timesonline.co.uk/tol/comment/faith/article4749183.ece.

13. James Sturcke, "Sharia Law in Canada, Almost," *The Guardian,* February 8, 2008, http://www.guardian.co.uk/news/blog/2008/feb/08/sharialawincanadaalmost; Meghan Wood, "Quebec Strikes Down Sharia Law," *Canadian Christianity,* http://www.canadianchristianity.com/cgi-bin/na.cgi?nationalupdates/050602quebec.

14. Lauren Russell, "Church Plans Koran-burning Event," *CNN,* July 30, 2010, http://articles.cnn.com/2010-07-29/us/florida.burn.quran.day_1_quran-burning -florida-church-terry-jones-american-muslims-religion?_s=PM:US.

15. Annie Gowen, "Far From Ground Zero, Other Plans for Mosques Run Into Vehement Opposition," *Washington Post,* August 23, 2010, http://www.washingtonpost .com/wp-dyn/content/article/2010/08/22/AR2010082202895_2.html?sid= ST2010082202944.

16. See my book, *The Coming Great Calamity* (Nampa, ID: Pacific Press®, 1997).

17. White, *The Great Controversy,* 590.

18. Ellen G. White, *Last Day Events* (Nampa, ID: Pacific Press®, 1992), 129.

PART 3

Misunderstandings About the Delay

CHAPTER 12

Expectations

My wife, Lois, scared me one night. I expected her to be home by around nine o'clock, but she didn't show up then. At first, I wasn't concerned about the delay in her return, but by 10:00 P.M., I was beginning to get worried; and when 10:30 came and went, I reached a level of extreme anxiety. I decided that if she didn't arrive by eleven o'clock, I would call the police and ask if there'd been any accidents in the area. I had just picked up the phone when she walked through the front door. I breathed a huge sigh of relief, and she apologized for not taking her cell phone with her.

Expectations are always about the future. We can't expect something to happen that has already happened. Sometimes expectations have to do with what we anticipate will occur at a particular time in the future, such as my expectation that Lois would show up by nine o'clock. In other situations, our expectations have to do with what we think will result from a particular action on our part or someone else's part. Most people enter into marriage expecting a blissful future together. The high divorce rate in the United States is a clear indication that many of those expectations are misplaced. Perhaps we should just do away with all expectations—that way we wouldn't feel disappointed when the future doesn't turn out the way we had anticipated.

But we can't do that—we can't avoid looking to the future and trying to discern how we should relate to it. We *have* to make plans for tomorrow. Just today—the day I'm writing these words—I swallowed hard and charged a little more than two thousand dollars on my credit card for a plane ticket to India six months from now. I knew that the longer I waited, the more people would make reservations ahead of me, the harder it would be to get the schedule I wanted, and the higher the fare would be. Furthermore, I wanted Lois to go with me using a frequent flyer ticket, and the longer one waits, the more difficult those are to book. Fortunately, I got just what I wanted for both tickets.

In charging that two thousand dollars to my credit card, I demonstrated my expectation that six months from now I will be healthy enough to take the trip and that the planes will be flying to India. You may say that of course I should expect the planes to be flying to India in six months; most flights do depart and arrive on time.* However, thousands of airline passengers had their trips canceled or postponed for about week after the attack on New York City's Twin Towers in September 2001; thousands more experienced week-long delays as a result of the Eyjafjallajökull† volcanic eruption in Iceland in April 2010; and in late December 2010, severe snowstorms in the United States and Europe caused the cancellation of hundreds of flights on each continent *just at Christmastime*! In each of these situations, thousands of passengers were stuck in airports for several days as they waited for the airlines to reschedule their flights.

These, of course, are fairly rare situations. But weather and mechanical problems cause delayed and canceled flights every day. So while the airlines make every effort to fly on schedule, thus meeting our expectations, they can't guarantee that every flight will be on time.

Expectations are typically either about our fears or our wishes. In the majority of cases, our fearful expectations about the future turn out to have been groundless, and more often than not our wishes are fulfilled,

---

* Update after the trip: My flight from San Francisco to Boise was canceled, which delayed my arrival back home by almost twelve hours. All other flights departed and arrived on time.

† Don't feel bad—I can't pronounce it either!

especially if we've planned carefully. But when a wish isn't met, disappointment is the inevitable result. Sometimes the realization that our expectations won't be met creeps up on us gradually, and sometimes it crashes upon us with a bang. Often it's a combination of both: We may go along for some time with the uncomfortable feeling that what we're expecting won't happen, but we so much *want* it to be true that we keep finding reasons to believe it *is* true. Then, suddenly, something happens, and we can no longer deny the truth: our expectation won't be fulfilled. And with that comes disappointment. And the longer we resisted acknowledging the truth, the more bitter the disappointment is.

Spiritual expectations

There are many ways in which God's people set themselves up for disappointment in their spiritual lives because what they expected to happen didn't. Abraham, whose story I reviewed in chapter 1, is a prime example. God called Abraham out of Ur of the Chaldees with the promise that all the world would be blessed through his descendants. Over a period of several years, God became increasingly specific about the fact that Abraham would have a son. However, God didn't tell Abraham *when* that son would be born.

If I had been Abraham, I'm sure I would have expected the child to be born most any time, especially given the fact that Sarah was nearing menopause. That, indeed, is exactly what Abraham believed, and he became increasingly anxious as the years rolled by and no son was born. He even told God what would happen if the son didn't show up fairly soon: his head servant would inherit his estate. That's when God became very specific about what He planned. He said, "A son who is your own flesh and blood will be your heir" (Genesis 15:4). However, more time passed, and Sarah still didn't become pregnant. Finally, in desperation, Abraham agreed to Sarah's proposal that he have a son by her handmaid. And, as you know, the world is still suffering from the conflict between those two sons.* Abraham's false expectation that God planned to give him a son

---

* Abraham's son Isaac became father of the Jews, and his son Ishmael became father of the Arabs.

in the immediate future had a major spiritual consequence not only for him but also for the whole world.

Unfulfilled religious expectations are still causing damage to the spiritual lives of God's people. Some people expect that when they're baptized, all their temptations will go away and God will give them immediate victory over all their sins. So when they fall into sin, they become very discouraged—some even giving up their faith. But the problem isn't with God or Christianity. The problem is their unrealistic expectations about what would happen when they became Christians.

What should Christians expect to have happen when they pray? Some people expect an overpowering, ecstatic feeling to wash over them, and when that doesn't happen, they question whether their prayers are genuine.

Some people's expectations about what will happen when they walk into a church for the first time pose a significant spiritual danger. They expect that everyone will smile and welcome them with open arms, and when no one smiles, asks their names, and tells them how glad they are to have them visit the church, they feel that the church has been cold and unfriendly and has rejected them, and they never go back. Or perhaps the church welcomed them when they first began to attend, and they joined, but then someone criticized them, and they felt hurt and left.

Please understand: it's right to believe that every visitor in every church should be welcomed with open arms and that no one should criticize them. That's how every church *ought* to be. But we live in a world of imperfect humans, and, unfortunately, these expectations aren't always met. So, it's important not to expect too much of any church.

Another danger has to do with unrealistic expectations about God's love. When Christians experience a particularly difficult situation, there's always the temptation to ask why: Why did God allow my home to burn down? Why did God allow me to lose my job? Why did God allow my husband, my wife, or my child to die? Why did God allow me to have a terrible accident or to come down with this fatal disease? The unstated expectation in such a situation is that if God truly loved us, He would protect us and our loved ones from all harm. But that's an unrealistic expectation. Bad things *do* happen to good people.

Some people ask God for a sign. They "put out a fleece," and they expect a good result when they follow the direction they believe the "fleece" indicated. When they don't get that good result, they blame God for letting them down. Their expectation of what would happen hasn't been met, and they're disappointed. However, the problem is their expectations, not God's leading.

Ideally, all Christians would have realistic expectations about all aspects of their life, but none of us do. All of us have disappointments that test our faith because what we expected to have happen didn't happen. However, those who hang in there with God discover that those unmet expectations provide them with opportunities to grow in their understanding of how the Christian life works and how God leads in their lives. The result is a more mature, more peaceful spiritual experience.

It's critically important for pastors and teachers to give the people they instruct a realistic understanding of what to expect of God and their fellow Christians. I suspect that many an immature Christian has succumbed to spiritual damage caused by unrealistic portrayals of the Christian life that they heard from the pulpit or in the classroom. However, it wouldn't be fair for us to pin all the blame for unrealistic expectations on pastors and teachers. Since everyone has unrealistic spiritual expectations of one kind or another, it's important for each of us to cultivate a spiritual maturity that can carry us through the crises they create.

Eschatological expectations

Eschatology is a theological term that means the study of end-time events, the second coming of Christ, and the establishment of God's eternal kingdom. And eschatological expectations are among the critical spiritual expectations that Christians need to be aware of. It's extremely important that our eschatological expectations be realistic, because the failure of unrealistic eschatological expectations can be devastating to our spiritual experience.

Old Testament eschatology centered on the coming of the promised Messiah. The prophets wrote a great deal about what the people of Israel could expect to happen when the Messiah came. Isaiah was especially prolific on this subject. He said, for example, that the Messiah would trample the nations in His anger, and pour out their blood on the ground (Isaiah 63:6). Isaiah also said that Israel would be exalted above all the nations:

> In the last days
>   the mountain of the LORD's temple [Jerusalem] will be established
>   as highest of the mountains [the nations];
> it will be exalted above the hills,
>   and all nations will stream to it.
> Many peoples will come and say,
>   "Come, let us go up to the mountain of the LORD,
>   to the temple of the God of Jacob" (Isaiah 2:2, 3).

Think of what this meant to the Jewish people when Jesus was living on earth. They were smarting under the thumb of the Roman Empire. A Roman governor controlled their nation politically, and he even largely controlled appointments to the priesthood. Gone was the glory that Israel had enjoyed during the reigns of David and Solomon. Naturally, the people and their leaders longed for those "good old days." And as they listened to what the Old Testament prophets said, they heard that the Messiah would defeat the nations around them and make their nation chief in all the world.

They were familiar also with the prophecies of Daniel, including chapter 9, which stated that the Messiah would appear 490 years after a Persian governor issued a decree restoring the Jews to their homeland after their Babylonian captivity. This decree was also to have authorized the rebuilding of their temple and to have granted them a measure of political independence. While no doubt there was some uncertainty about which decree Daniel had in mind,* there was a widespread expectancy generally

---

* Cyrus issued a decree permitting the Jews to return to Jerusalem and rebuild their temple. Darius issued two such decrees, as did Artaxerxes. I discuss the interpretation of Daniel 9 at length in chapters 23–27 of my book *The Case for the Investigative Judgment.*

that the time of the Messiah's appearing was near, and they understood this to mean that the Messiah would soon lead the armies of Israel to defeat the hated Romans. Soon Israel would be established as the greatest nation on the earth. Soon all other nations would be subservient to them! How the leaders in Israel must have relished the hope that they would be the ones to assist the Messiah in conquering the Romans and setting up His eternal kingdom on earth!

This exaltation of Israel was their expectation—and it was their problem. Speaking of these Jewish leaders, Ellen White said that "when Christ came in a manner contrary to their *expectations,* they would not receive Him."[1] The spiritual consequences of the false expectations of the Jewish leaders can hardly be overemphasized!

There are at least three reasons why the Jewish leaders rejected Jesus. One was their misinterpretation of the prophecies. "The Jews had the Old Testament Scriptures and supposed themselves conversant with them. But they made a woeful mistake. The prophecies that refer to the glorious second appearing of Christ in the clouds of heaven they regarded as referring to His first coming. Because He did not come according to their *expectations,* they turned away from Him."[2]

Another reason why the Jews rejected Jesus was their rigid adherence to religious tradition: "Christ's mission was not understood by the people of His time. The manner of His coming was not in accordance with their *expectations.* . . . The Jews had exalted the forms and ceremonies [of their religion] and had lost sight of their object. The traditions, maxims, and enactments of men hid from them the lessons which God intended to convey. . . . When the Reality came, in the person of Christ, they did not recognize in Him the fulfillment of all their types, the substance of all their shadows."[3]

A third reason the Jews rejected Jesus was the ambitious pride of their leaders. "The Jewish leaders had studied the teachings of the prophets concerning the kingdom of the Messiah; but they had done this, not with a sincere desire to know the truth, but with the purpose of finding evidence to sustain their ambitious hopes. When Christ came in a manner contrary to their *expectations,* they would not receive Him; and in order to justify themselves, they tried to prove Him a deceiver."[4]

It wasn't just the Jewish leaders who held these false expectations about the Messiah. The entire culture was infected with this unrealistic hope. John the Baptist, the very forerunner of the Messiah, "did not understand the nature of Christ's kingdom. He *expected* Jesus to take the throne of David; and as time passed, and the Saviour made no claim to kingly authority, John became perplexed and troubled. . . . There were hours when the whisperings of demons tortured his spirit, and the shadow of a terrible fear crept over him. Could it be that the long-hoped-for Deliverer had not yet appeared?"[5] False expectations regarding the Messiah caused deep spiritual anguish to God's own ordained prophet!

Christ's disciples, too, held the erroneous view that the Messiah would lead the armies of Israel to defeat the Romans. Ellen White commented that when Christ spoke to them about His coming death, they "did not comprehend His words. The glory seemed far away. Their eyes were fixed upon the nearer view, the earthly life of poverty, humiliation, and suffering. Must their glowing *expectations* of the Messiah's kingdom be relinquished? Were they not to see their Lord exalted to the throne of David?"[6]

Even after Christ's resurrection, the disciples clung to the false expectations that He would lead the nation of Israel to victory over Rome and establish His own kingdom of glory. This is evident from their question to Him just before He ascended to heaven: "Lord, are you at this time going to restore the kingdom to Israel?" (Acts 1:6). So, it's very obvious that people can easily misinterpret and misunderstand the Bible's eschatological prophecies. It's also obvious that the spiritual implications of such misunderstandings can be extremely serious. This lesson from the Jews of Christ's day should warn us to be very careful how we interpret the Bible's eschatological prophecies for our day lest we also misinterpret them and reap the consequences of that misunderstanding.

False expectations of the Second Coming

The most notable misinterpretation of prophecy in the past couple of hundred years was William Miller's claim that the 2,300 days of Daniel

8:14 would end with Christ's second coming in 1844. Hiram Edson said that when Jesus didn't come when they expected Him, "our fondest hopes and *expectations* were blasted."[7] "We wept, and wept, till the day dawn."[8]

However, I believe there's a significant difference between the Jewish misinterpretation of the prophecies regarding Christ's first coming and the Millerite misunderstanding of Daniel's prophecy of the 2,300 days. Ellen White explained the reason for their misunderstanding: "God designed to prove His people. His hand covered a mistake in the reckoning of the prophetic periods. Adventists did not discover their error, nor was it discovered by the most learned of their opponents."[9]

Of course, this doesn't mean that Miller's opponents *did* interpret the prophecy about the 2,300 days correctly. Ellen White went on to point out that they said, " '[Miller's] reckoning of the prophetic periods is correct. Some great event is about to take place, but it is not what Mr. Miller predicts; it is the conversion of the world, not the second advent of Christ.' "[10] Surely, world history since 1844 has shattered any expectation of the conversion of the whole world!

So what about us? Is there a danger that we might misinterpret the prophecies about the final crisis, the time of trouble, and Christ's second coming?

Misinterpretation of the end time is already happening in a significant way among many Protestant Christians. The theory of a secret rapture in which "the church" will be taken out of the world prior to the "the tribulation" is a major misinterpretation of the biblical evidence about Christ's second coming, and the spiritual implications are enormous. What will those who *expect* a pretribulation rapture do when it becomes obvious that the final crisis has come upon the world and nobody has been taken to heaven? The most dangerous part of the rapture theory is that it lulls Christians into thinking that they don't need to put forth a major effort to deal with their character defects, because, after all, they won't have to pass through the time of trouble that will test the character of all who remain on the earth.

But what about Seventh-day Adventists? Are we in danger of being misled by false interpretations of end-time events despite all the instruction we've been given in both the Bible and the writings of Ellen White? That will be the topic of the next three chapters.

1. White, *The Desire of Ages,* 212; the italics in this and the following E. G. White quotations have been added for emphasis.

2. Ellen G. White, *Christ Triumphant* (Hagerstown, MD: Review and Herald®, 1999), 342.

3. Ellen G. White, *Christ's Object Lessons* (Hagerstown, MD: Review and Herald®, 1941), 34, 35.

4. White, *The Desire of Ages,* 212.

5. Ellen G. White, *Conflict and Courage* (Hagerstown, MD: Review and Herald®, 1970), 277.

6. White, *The Desire of Ages,* 417, 418.

7. Hiram Edson, fragment of a manuscript on his "Life and Experience," cited in *Seventh-day Adventist Encyclopedia* (Hagerstown, MD: Review and Herald®, 1966), 364; emphasis added.

8. Hiram Edson, cited in George R. Knight, *A Brief History of Seventh-day Adventists* (Hagerstown, MD: Review and Herald®, 1999), 25.

9. Ellen G. White, *The Story of Redemption* (Hagerstown, MD: Review and Herald®, 1947), 362, 363.

10. White, *The Story of Redemption,* 363.

CHAPTER 13

A Dangerous Expectation: Dating the Second Coming

The Millerites were hardly the first people to set a date for Christ's second coming. In fact, we find the first recorded instance of speculation about the time of Christ's return in the New Testament. After Peter affirmed that he loved Jesus, the Lord said that like Him, Peter would die by crucifixion. The ever-impulsive Peter pointed to "the disciple Jesus loved," that is, John, and said to Jesus, "Lord, what about him?" (John 21:21). Jesus replied, "If I want him to remain alive until I return, what is that to you?" (verse 22). John wrote that based on this exchange, "the rumor spread among the brothers that this disciple would not die" (verse 23). In other words, some people thought that Jesus meant He would return before John died. John himself put that rumor to rest. He pointed out that "Jesus did not say that he [John] would not die; he only said, 'If I want him to remain alive until I return, what is that to you?' " (verse 23).

Setting dates for Christ's return has a long history!

Indeed it does! In researching the topic of this chapter, I Googled "predictions about the end of the world," and the very first Web address on the list, the "Library of Date Setters of the End of the World!!!" listed more than 220 end-time predictions that have been made during the Christian era—all of them failures![1] I'll share a few examples.

Date setting during the past two thousand years

In the previous chapter, I said that the Jews of Christ's time were quite aware that the 490 years of Daniel 9:24 were about to expire, and there was a great deal of excitement about the coming of the Messiah. While the Jews' understanding of how the Messiah would come and the role He would play was quite different from ours, their mind-set and ours generate pretty much the same excitement. And that mind-set easily lends itself to extremism and fanaticism.

Numerous self-proclaimed messiahs arose among the Jews during the first century A.D., including Barabbas, on whose cross Christ was crucified.* In a speech Gamaliel made to caution the Sanhedrin against taking drastic action against the early disciples, he mentioned a man by the name of Theudas who proclaimed himself the Messiah and rebelled against the Roman government (see Acts 5:36). According to Josephus, Theudas was beheaded, many of his followers were also killed, and the rest were scattered.[2]

Hippolytus, a prominent Christian theologian who lived from about A.D. 170 to 235, wrote a vivid account of the events preceding the end of the world,[3] which he calculated would occur about two hundred years after his time.[4] A Roman priest and theologian who lived toward the end of the second and the beginning of the third century predicted that Christ would return in A.D. 500, basing his conclusions on the dimensions of Noah's ark!

Millennial fever seems to have gripped people who lived near the end of the first millennium in the same way it did those living near the end of the second millennium. (Remember Y2K?) Shortly before the year 1000, a monk by the name of Abbo of Fleury claimed to have heard a preacher who said that the antichrist would be unleashed in the year 1000 and the last judgment would soon follow. A solar eclipse set off a panic in the German army of Emperor Otto I because the soldiers thought the eclipse was a sign of the end of the world. And Otto III, had Charlemagne's body exhumed on Pentecost in the year 1000, supposedly in order to forestall the apocalypse!

---

* Barabbas is not mentioned in the "Library of Date Setters" Web site.

The "Library of Date Setters" Web site states that the year 1000

> goes down as one of the most pronounced states of hysteria over
> the return of Christ. All members of society seemed affected by the
> prediction that Jesus was coming back on Jan 1, 1000 AD There
> really weren't any of the events required by the Bible transpiring at
> that time. The magical number 1000 was primarily the sole reason
> for the expectation. During December 999 AD, everyone was on
> their best behavior; worldly goods were sold and given to the poor,
> swarms of pilgrims headed east to meet the Lord at Jerusalem,
> buildings went unrepaired, crops were left unplanted [shades of
> the Millerites!], and criminals were set free from jails. [But] the
> year 999 AD turned into 1000 AD and nothing happened.[5]

The Taborites were a religious community in the fifteenth century
that the Catholic Church considered heretical. They believed that once
their persecutors were defeated, Christ would return and rule the world
from Mount Tabor, a mountain south of Prague.

Another flurry of end-time predictions occurred in the wake of Martin
Luther's break with the Catholic Church. A radical reformer by the name
of Thomas Müntzer led a popular revolt by some three-hundred-thousand
peasants against the established government.[6] Müntzer announced that
Christ would return after he and his men had destroyed the high and the
mighty. It is estimated that, unfortunately, one hundred thousand of his
followers were killed during the ensuing war—and Christ didn't return.

In the early 1800s, Mary Bateman, a fortune-teller, claimed to have a
magic chicken that laid eggs with end-time messages on them, one of
which declared that Christ's coming was near!

Harold Camping, a radio broadcaster and the president of Family
Stations, Inc., set off a frenzy of end-time enthusiasm in 2010 and 2011.
Camping's intensive study of the Bible led him to the firm conviction
that "beyond a shadow of a doubt, May 21, 2011, will be the date of the
Rapture and the judgment." He even went so far as to say that "if May
21 passes and I'm still here, that means I wasn't saved."[7]

This wasn't Camping's first venture into date setting. In 1992, he published a book titled *1994?* in which he stated that "abundant Biblical information focuses on 1994 as the likely end of the world."[8] Though the world didn't end in 1994, Camping was even more certain that Christ would return on his new, very specific date of May 21, 2011.

Camping's newest theory captured the imagination of thousands of Christians in the United States and other parts of the world. Mary Exley of Colorado Springs, Colorado, a thirty-two-year-old army veteran who did two stints in Iraq, devoted herself to promoting Camping's prediction. "We're commanded by God to warn people," she said. "I wish I could be like everyone else, but it's so much better to know that when the end comes, you'll be safe."

Exley organized caravans of RVs to carry the warning of Christ's soon return from city to city. It was posted on billboards in cities from Bridgeport, Connecticut, to Little Rock, Arkansas. She and others traveled to Latin America and Africa to carry "the message," and she said, "I don't really have plans to come back. Time is short."

Of course, May 21, 2011, passed without leaving any evidence of a rapture or of the arrival of the Judgment Day.

Finally, there's the so-called Mayan calendar with its "prophetic" date of December 21, 2012, that's being trumpeted even more by New Agers and other non-Christians than by Christians. Hollywood even produced a movie about it, *2012,* which pictured towering tsunamis and global earthquakes that collapsed skyscrapers in cities all over the world. I did a Google search of "December 21, 2012," and came up with 29.8 million hits. End-of-the-world predictions abound!

Adventist date setters

I hardly need to recount the story of William Miller and October 22, 1844, to Adventist readers.[9] Perhaps not as well known is the fact that after 1844, some Millerites speculated that Christ would return on October 22, 1845—among them, James White. He dropped this idea on the advice of Ellen Harmon, whom he married about a year later. Others weren't so wise: disappointed Millerites predicted Christ's return in 1846, and then in 1849, and then in 1850, 1851, 1854, 1866, and 1877![10]

Joseph Bates based his belief that Christ would return in 1851 on the seven "times" that the priest in the earthly sanctuary was supposed to sprinkle blood upon the altar on the Day of Atonement. The Millerites, and Seventh-day Adventists after them, understood the words *time* and *times* in Daniel 7:25 to refer to *years,* which was what prompted Bates to interpret the seven *times* the blood was sprinkled to mean that Christ would return seven years *after* 1844—in other words, in 1851. At the time, some Sabbath keeping Adventists took Bates's suggestion seriously, until Ellen White published instruction from the Lord that Bates was wrong. Bates then dropped his theory, sparing the infant church more disappointment and disillusionment.[11]

But Adventist date setting didn't end with Bates. Over the years, various Adventists have developed date-setting schemes based on various time periods in the Bible. The Israelites' forty-year wilderness wandering prompted some to suggest Christ would return in 1884.[12] And Jesus' statement that "this generation will certainly not pass away until all these things have happened" (Matthew 24:34) was the basis of a flurry of end-time expectation in the 1930s, since no member of the generation that saw the falling of the stars would have lived beyond that time.

I began my ministerial internship in 1961 in Pomona, California, and I can still remember the pastor of the church preaching a fiery sermon in which he said that Christ would surely come back in 1964. His conclusion was based on the 120 years that it took Noah to build the ark. The math is quite simple: 1844 plus 120 equals 1964. Several years ago I received a letter from an Adventist woman who assured me that Christ would return in 2027 because that would be two thousand years from the time of His baptism in A.D. 27!

The jubilee theory prompted some Adventists to expect either Christ's second coming or at least the beginning of the time of trouble in 1994. The math is more complex than adding forty years or 120 years to 1844, but it's still fairly understandable. According to Leviticus 25:8–13, there are forty-nine years in a jubilee. Daniel's prophecy of 490 years from the command to restore and build Jerusalem to the coming of Messiah the

Prince (Daniel 9:25) is almost certainly based on the jubilee cycle (49 x 10 = 490). Assuming that 457 B.C. was a jubilee year, the 490 years ended in A.D. 34, which would also be a jubilee year. Counting forty jubilees from A.D. 34 brings us to 1994—hence the expectation in some Adventist circles that 1994 was the date for Christ's return or perhaps the close of probation or the beginning of the final crisis.

Recently, I received a newsletter from an Adventist independent ministry that gave very specific dates for several end-time events that are supposed to occur in 2013. The author stated that the latter rain will descend on those prepared to receive it on May 15, probation will close on September 14, the first six plagues will be poured out between September 15 and 21, the seventh plague will fall on September 22, and Christ will return on September 23.[13] Wow!

There's also the six-thousand-year theory. Quite a number of Adventists speculated that Jesus would return during or near the year 2000, since, according to Ussher's chronology of biblical history, that would be six thousand years after Creation. A few years ago, some Adventists were pointing to a number of statements Ellen White made in which she speaks of the history of sin on our planet lasting about six thousand years. She said, for example, that "the great controversy between Christ and Satan, that has been carried on for almost six thousand years, is soon to close."[14] Some people concluded that this meant Jesus should come about the year 2000. Of course, that didn't happen.

A time-setting scheme of sorts that a number of individuals have told me about in the last twenty years is based on Revelation 17:9–11, which says that the seven heads of the beast on which the harlot of verse 1 sits "are also seven kings. Five have fallen, one is, the other has not yet come; but when he does come, he must remain for a little while. The beast who once was, and now is not, is an eighth king. He belongs to the seven and is going to his destruction." According to this theory, the eight kings mentioned in these verses represent the last eight popes who reign before Christ's second coming. So, which pope starts this sequence? The Vatican and the government of Benito Mussolini signed a concordat in 1929 called the Lateran Treaty that gave the Vatican independent political rule over 108 acres in Rome. Those who support this interpretation start the countdown of popes with the year of that treaty. Here's the list of popes:

Pius XI (1922–1939)
Pius XII (1939–1958)
John XXIII (1958–1963)
Paul XI (1963–1978)
John Paul I (1978)
John Paul II (1978–2005)
Benedict XVI (2005–)

That's seven popes. Benedict is quite elderly, which probably means that he won't be a pope much longer. The eighth pope, still to be elected, is supposed to reign only a short time, and then—well, what then? Revelation simply says this eighth king "is going to his destruction."

I believe that this theory is pure speculation. There isn't a shred of an exegetical basis for interpreting the eight kings of Revelation 16:9–11 as representing popes, and there's certainly nothing to suggest 1929 as the year with which to begin the countdown. Interpreting it in this way is simply one more way to draw people into believing that Jesus' second coming is just around the corner.

Now, you know from reading up to this point in this book that I find significant evidence for believing that the second coming of Christ is near. But this evidence has to do with trends in the world that are clearly fulfillments of certain basic biblical predictions about the condition of the world at the end of time. I am confident that the world is moving toward history's final events. But you also know from reading up to this point that God's plans develop slowly. Four thousand years elapsed between the time God told Adam that the woman's Seed would bruise the serpent's head and the time when Jesus actually was incarnated, and another two thousand years have passed since then. During this time, each generation has hoped—and many have believed—that theirs would be the generation to see Christ's coming.

My mother was born in Kansas in 1905, and her family moved to northwestern Wyoming when she was only about five years old. My mother told me that when she was about ten years old, she said to her mother one day, "Mama, I wonder who I will marry when I grow up. Maybe he lives way down in Texas!" Her mother replied, "Oh, honey, you'll never get married. Jesus will come before you're old enough for that." My mother did indeed marry a Texan, and she bore two children, who gave her six grandchildren—and she died in 1996 at the ripe old age of ninety-one.

Back in 1955 or 1956, I was standing beside the water fountain in the lobby of Hamilton Hall, the men's dormitory at what was then Southwestern Junior College, chatting with a fellow theology student. We got to talking about the second coming of Christ, and he assured me that by all means, Jesus would come within the next five years.

A little later, when I was a pastor in the wind-blown town of Mojave, California, I preached a sermon in which I told my small congregation that I believed it was possible that Christ would return sometime in the next twenty-five years. After the service, one of the women in the church protested. "Pastor," she said, "Jesus is going to come much sooner than in twenty-five years!" I pointed out that I had said "*sometime* in the next twenty-five years," and if He came in five or ten years, that would be within the timeframe I suggested. She was relieved at that. However, nearly fifty years have passed since then, and Jesus still has not returned.

Every now and then someone tells someone else about an event he or she anticipates experiencing within the next five or ten years—graduation from college, retirement, meeting a long-range job goal, and so on—and the person he or she is talking to remarks, "I hope we're in heaven by then." I'm sure you've heard this said and perhaps have said it yourself. I have. Yet even this mild form of time setting can have dangerous consequences. Kenneth Wade, in his book *Jesus for a New Millennium,* told the following story:

> Years ago when I was in college, my wife told me about a visit she'd had with an elderly gentleman who had lost his hope. "When I was a young boy," he told her, "I expected Jesus to come any day. I've been hoping He'd come for the past eighty years. But now I don't believe it anymore. I just can't believe it. It's been too long."[15]

I think I'm safe in assuming that this man didn't invent the notion of Christ's return being "within the next five years." So, who put it in his head? It was the well-meaning parents, Sabbath School teachers, church school teachers, and preachers in his life. When you and I talk about Jesus surely coming "in the next five years," we plant the same seeds in the minds of our children and young people and even in the minds of spiritually immature adults. And one day those seeds are likely to sprout into the same spiritual tragedy as that of the old man in Kenneth Wade's story. Christ's warning is just as relevant today as it was two thousand years ago: "About that day or hour no one knows" (Matthew 24:36). Date setting is one of the dangers that extreme expectations about the end time can lead to. And the spiritual dangers are very real indeed!

1. http://www.bible.ca/pre-date-setters.htm. Unless otherwise referenced, the examples of date setting prior to William Miller are from the list on this Web site.

2. http://en.wikipedia.org/wiki/Theudas.

3. http://en.wikipedia.org/wiki/Hippolytus_of_Rome#Legends.

4. http://www.bible.ca/pre-date-setters.htm.

5. http://www.bible.ca/pre-date-setters.htm.

6. http://en.wikipedia.org/wiki/German_Peasants%27_War#Social_and _economic_conditions_in_the_late_15th_century.

7. Tom Breen, "End of Days in May? Believers Enter Final Stretch," *MSNBC*, January 3, 2011, http://www.msnbc.msn.com/id/40885541/ns/us_news-life/t/end-days -may-believers-enter-final-stretch/.

8. Harold Camping, *1994?* (New York: Vantage Press, 1992), back cover.

9. For an overview, see chapter 14 of my book *Challenges to the Remnant* (Nampa, ID: Pacific Press®, 2008), 125–137.

10. See Spalding, *Origin and History of Seventh-day Adventists,* 1:145, 146.

11. Ibid.

12. I can't cite a source for this, but I *have* read it, and I have talked with others who said they had read it too.

13. Unfortunately, I discarded the newsletter without noting any of the facts of publication.

14. White, *The Great Controversy,* 518; see also pages 88, 656, 658, and 659.

15. Kenneth Wade, *Jesus for a New Millennium* (Nampa, ID: Pacific Press®, 2000), 12.

CHAPTER 14

A Dangerous Expectation: Sunday Laws

Sunday laws have been a part of the Adventist eschatological scenario since the late 1840s. The first person to suggest that the mark of the beast in Revelation 13:16, 17 represented the legal enforcement in the United States of Sunday as a day of rest and worship was Joseph Bates. In a pamphlet published in January 1847, titled *The Seventh-day Sabbath a Perpetual Sign,* he said,

> There are tens of thousands that are looking for Jesus, that dont [*sic*] believe the above doctrines [1844, the remnant, the law, the Sabbath, etc.], what will become of them? Consult John, he knows better than we do; he has only described two companies. See xiv:9-11, 12. One is keeping the commandments and faith of Jesus. The other has the mark of the beast. How? . . . Is it not clear that the first day of the week for the Sabbath or holy day, is the mark of the beast?[1]

The following year James and Ellen White endorsed Bates's views in a pamphlet titled *A Word to the Little Flock* that they copublished. In this pamphlet, Ellen White said,

I saw all that "would not receive the mark of the Beast, and of his

Image, in their foreheads or in their hands," could not buy or sell. I saw that the number (666) of the Image Beast was made up; and that it was the beast that changed the Sabbath, and the Image Beast had followed on after, and kept the Pope's, and not God's Sabbath. And all we were required to do, was to give up God's Sabbath, and keep the Pope's, and then we should have the mark of the Beast, and of his Image.[2]

Throughout her lifetime, Ellen White continued to expand on this primitive understanding of the mark of the beast. In *The Great Controversy,* her magnum opus on end-time events, she went into great detail about Sunday legislation being the final violation of God's law by an apostate world. She made it ultraclear that during the final crisis, the United States will enact Sunday legislation that, under the influence of demonic forces, will in time spread around the globe.[3] And she said that these laws will foster intense persecution against God's people.

Given the essential role Sunday legislation plays in Ellen White's end-time scenario, those who accept her prophetic ministry must expect that Sunday laws will be enacted and enforced in the United States and around the world.

Sunday laws in the late 1800s

The first edition of *The Great Controversy* was published in 1888, and it was during this very time—the late 1880s and early 1890s—that several southern states began to enforce their Sunday laws strictly. As a result, a number of Seventh-day Adventists were prosecuted. The first, Samuel Mitchel, of Quitman, Georgia, spent thirty days in a county jail on a charge of violating a Sunday law. However, the enforcement was harshest in Tennessee. In 1885, three Adventists who lived in that state—William Dortch, W. H. Parker, and James Stem—were fined and imprisoned, spending several weeks on a chain gang. In 1889, and again in 1890, R. M. King was arrested for plowing corn and hoeing his potato patch on Sunday. Three years later, five Adventists were brought to trial for violating Tennessee's Sunday ordinance. They also spent time working on a chain gang.

During this same period, advocates of Sunday legislation succeeded in having several bills introduced in the United States Congress. One of their chief allies was H. W. Blair, a Republican senator from New Hampshire. In 1888, Blair introduced a bill intended "To Secure to the People the Enjoyment of the First Day of the Week, Commonly Known as the Lord's Day, as a Day of Rest, and to Promote Its Observance as a Day of Religious Worship." This bill was defeated in large part because of the vigorous opposition of the Seventh-day Adventist Church under the fiery leadership of Alonzo T. Jones.

It's understandable that Seventh-day Adventist end-time hopes were aroused to a fever pitch during the late 1880s and early 1890s. Ellen White had just published *The Great Controversy,* and events transpiring in the southern United States and in the United States Congress seemed to be fulfilling her scenario. The end was in sight! Jesus would come in just a few more years—hallelujah!

What about Sunday laws today?

After about 1895, though, the enforcement of Sunday laws died down, and ever since, these laws have been disappearing from the American scene. This has been very puzzling to Seventh-day Adventists, because for 150 years we have viewed Sunday observance as the key apostasy of the Christian world during the end time, and we have seen Sunday laws as the preeminent sign of the approaching end of the world.

Adventists have responded to the demise of Sunday laws in three ways. By far the majority of us have simply trusted that the final crisis, including Sunday laws, *will come* in God's good time. However, there have been two more extreme responses. Unfortunately, a significant number of Adventists, in their anxiety to see evidence of the final crisis and the nearness of Christ's return, have tended to interpret every hint of a Sunday law in some obscure American village as a sign that the end is upon us. Usually the language in the literature published by this segment of Adventism is shrill and alarmist. We are warned that the agitation for a Sunday ordinance in Podunkville is sure evidence that the final crisis can't be much more than six months away. An example of this kind of thinking is an e-mail I recieved on August 11, 2011, from an individual who was commenting on the Catholic Church's support for a Sunday law that is already on the books in North Dakota. He said that this is "more evidence that Jesus' coming is soon."

This kind of thinking is very unrealistic. It overlooks the fact that the final crisis will be global, not local. It forgets that the platform of religious conservatives who happen to dominate local politics is a far cry from the national and international emergency that will bring on the final crisis. It fails to take into account that Ellen White pointed to a change in the Constitution of the United States rather than to a Sunday law in a state or local community as a clear sign of the end.

Shortly after I completed this chapter, I was chatting with the president of a conference in India about a mission trip that my wife and I planned to take in late February and early March 2011, and, in the course of the conversation, he said, "Pastor Moore, what do you know about the agreement between Obama and the papacy over the passage of a Sunday law in the United States?" I had never heard of such a thing, so I asked him where he got the information. "Oh," he said, "it was in a letter sent out by General Conference President Ted Wilson. I received an e-mail about it."

I was immediately suspicious that the whole thing was a false rumor about Sunday laws and end-time events perpetrated by some misguided Adventist who had more enthusiasm than common sense. However, I promised my friend that I would check it out and get back to him.

The next day I called the General Conference and spoke with both Elder Wilson's secretary and someone who worked in the General Conference Communication Department. Both told me that they had received numerous phone calls about this letter, and it did not exist. So I urge that the next time you receive an alarmist e-mail about Sunday laws, please, *please,* check it out with the General Conference Communication Department before you pass it along.

Unfortunately, some Adventists have begun to take the opposite response to the waning of Sunday laws. They say Ellen White's prediction of end-time Sunday laws arose out of events transpiring around her at the time she wrote *The Great Controversy.* They suggest that the scenario she presented then is how the final conflict would have developed had it transpired in her day, but now that a hundred years have passed, it will likely revolve around other issues.

I disagree with this view for a couple reasons. First is the fact that throughout her seventy years of prophetic ministry, Ellen White maintained her view that Revelation's mark of the beast symbolizes Sunday laws that will be enacted first in the United States, and from there, they will spread around the globe shortly before Christ's second coming. I am aware that occasionally, Ellen White spoke or wrote incorrectly about some insignificant detail. However, it's another thing entirely to say that she was incorrect on a key issue of prophetic interpretation that she held from the late 1840s till her death in 1915.

Second, while I'm not aware of any current push for Sunday legislation in the United States Congress, there's evidence that persuades me that such a push could indeed develop. Here's why I believe it's still possible.

Why it could happen

First, back in 1961—fifty years ago as I write these words—the United States Supreme Court ruled that today's Sunday laws do not violate the First Amendment to the Constitution. While acknowledging "the religious origin of these laws," "the justices said that today nonreligious arguments for Sunday closing [are being] heard more distinctly."[4] Thus, if the Congress were to enact a Sunday law today, that law would probably withstand a challenge on religious grounds, provided that its stated purpose was largely secular. And, as we shall see later in this chapter, even religionists today, both Protestant and Catholic, argue that Sunday laws are good for the family and workers' health.*

A second reason why I believe that Sunday laws are a realistic possibility today is the Catholic Church's support of such laws. Popes have spoken out in favor of Sunday laws several times in the past two hundred years— one of the most recent instances of their promotion of such laws being John Paul II's apostolic letter titled *Dies Domini* (Latin for "Day of the Lord"), which was promulgated on July 30, 1998. In this letter, John

---

* See the addendum at the end of this chapter.

Paul traces the origin of the Sabbath to Creation—contrary to the view of many Protestants, who insist that the Sabbath originated at Sinai. John Paul urges the faithful to keep Sunday, the Lord's Day, holy.[5]

More significantly, the letter supports civil legislation making Sunday a day of rest and worship. John Paul says, for example, that "my predecessor Pope Leo XIII in his Encyclical *Rerum Novarum* [Latin for "Of New Things"] spoke of Sunday rest as a worker's right which the state must guarantee," and "in the particular circumstances of our own time, Christians will naturally strive to ensure that civil legislation respects their duty to keep Sunday holy."[6]

In September 2010, Benedict XVI issued a letter to be read at the Seventh World Meeting of Families. In his letter, he urged Catholics to be faithful in their observance of Sunday. "It is therefore necessary," the pope said, "to reflect and commit ourselves to reconciling the demands and requirements of work with those of the family, and to recover the true significance of rest, especially on Sundays, the weekly Easter, the day of the Lord and the day of man, the day of the family, of the community and of solidarity."[7] While not a call for Sunday legislation per se, Benedict's letter underscores the importance the papacy ascribes to Sunday observance.

In the past few years, there have been several instances of Sunday laws being proposed and, in some cases, enacted by countries other than the United States. While it may sound strange, there's been a good bit of agitation in Israel for a five-day workweek of Monday through Friday, making Sunday one of the weekend days off. Debate on the issue reached the point that on July 4, 2011, Prime Minister Benjamin Netanyahu appointed a committee to make a decision about the workweek by sometime in the fall of 2011. Part of the controversy over making Sunday a work-free weekend day is the fact that many Muslims live in Israel, and their holy day is Friday. A Sabbath-Sunday weekend would force devout Muslims to choose between their jobs and their religious faith.[8]

Then on June 6, 2011, sixty-five civil society organizations, trade unions, and churches launched the European Sunday Alliance in Brussels. The alliance's purpose is to maintain the health, safety, and social integration of European workers, including the right to time for family, social and civil engagement, and culture. One of the expert speakers at the conference stated that "whatever set of data you look at, whatever aspects you factor in or leave aside, the result is always the same: Any person working on Sundays is negatively affected both in terms of health and safety." Note again the nonreligious reasons for mandating Sunday as a day of rest.[9]

A clause in the German constitution mandates that Sunday be a day of rest and "spiritual elevation." However, a number of German states have made exceptions that permit shopping on selected Sundays throughout the year. The city of Berlin approved of shopping on ten Sundays a year, including the four immediately prior to Christmas. But on the grounds that retail workers need protection from working on Sundays, the Roman Catholic Church together with a coalition of Protestants churches joined with organized labor to oppose this liberalization. Germany's highest court agreed, overturning the city of Berlin's liberal Sunday shopping policy.[10]

Croatia closes stores on Sundays

In July 2008, the Croatian parliament voted that beginning on January 1, 2009, stores in that country must close on Sundays. Stores in gas, bus, and train stations were exempted, as were bakeries, newsstands, and flower shops. The ban is also lifted during summer months and winter holidays. The Catholic Church lobbied in favor of the law, and since 90 percent of Croatia's population is Roman Catholic, the legislation passed easily.[11]

Back in December of 1987, the council of the European Community adopted a resolution titled "Safety, Hygiene and Health at Work" that established Sunday as a weekly rest day. (Note the secular reasons suggested by the title of this resolution for establishing a day of rest.) The resolution made no link between a worker's health and safety and the establishment of Sunday as a weekly rest day. In fact, this issue never came up in discussions about the resolution. However, in November 1993, the European Parliament issued a "Working Time Directive" stipulating that a minimum rest period for workers should "in principle include Sunday."[12]

Britain challenged this phrase in the European Court of Justice on the grounds that no satisfactory explanation had been given as to "why Sunday, as a weekly rest day, is more closely connected with the health and safety of workers than any other day of the week." The court agreed and annulled the sentence in the resolution that gave preference to Sunday as a legal rest day.[13]

As the Working Time Directive stands today, it requires that each worker (1) have a minimum daily rest period of eleven consecutive hours in every twenty-four; (2) have a rest break during work time if the worker is on duty for longer than six hours; and (3) have a minimum weekly rest period of twenty-four uninterrupted hours in each seven-day period.[14] Seventh-day Adventists are fully supportive of this directive, including the twenty-four uninterrupted hours for each seven days worked, because workers can negotiate with their employers regarding which twenty-four-hour segment they'll take off.

However, in February 2009, five members of the European Parliament introduced a declaration calling for the recognition of a work-free Sunday as "an essential pillar of the European Social Model and a part of the European cultural heritage." The declaration called attention to a survey that showed "the likelihood of sickness and absenteeism in establishments that work on Saturdays and Sundays is 1.3 times greater" than it is in those that don't require weekend work. And it called upon "the Member States and the EU institutions to protect Sunday, as a weekly rest day, in forthcoming national and EU working-time legislation in order to enhance the protection of workers' health and the reconciliation of work and family life."[15] Note again the totally secular arguments in favor of passing a Sunday closing law.

One Web site lists forty-four European organizations that support protecting Sunday as a work-free day.[16] The most significant support came from a coalition of German Protestant churches, the (Catholic) Commission of the Bishops' Conferences of the European Community (COMECE), and the Church of England.[17] The Catholic Church in particular pushed hard for the directive. The statement about the survey that revealed a greater likelihood of sickness and absenteeism in establishments that work on Saturdays and Sundays was in direct response to the court's ruling that there was no link between a worker's health and Sunday as the specific day of rest.[18]

The amendment was never put to a vote in the European Parliament—a fact that drew the ire of several European Catholic bishops. Piotr Mazurkiewicz of Poland, who is secretary general of COMECE, said that the protection of Sunday is " 'a cornerstone of the European social model and an issue of central importance for workers and their families.' "[19]

Conclusions

Naturally, Seventh-day Adventists became aware of these various pieces of legislation or proposed legislation, and, with each one, I received shrill newsletters and e-mail blasts assuring readers that the final crisis is upon us, probation is about to close, and Jesus is about to come.

Now, I want to see Jesus come and put an end to the suffering on our planet as much as anyone. However, I do not see any of the cases that I cited above as providing a sufficient reason to conclude that the final crisis lies in the immediate future.

I say this for several reasons: First, the Israeli "Sunday law" and the change to Europe's Working Time Directive are proposals, not actual enactments by any legislative body. Second, the likelihood of the change to Europe's Working Time Directive being voted by the European Parliament is next to zero. To even be brought to the floor of the parliament, a majority of the members (394) would have had to sign the declaration before May 7, 2009.[20] That didn't happen. Furthermore, Europe is even more secular than the United States, making it highly unlikely that half of the members of the European Parliament would ever support this proposal. And third, on the remote chance that the parliament should add the work-free Sunday to its Working Time Directive, that would be a *European* legislative enactment, not an *American* one.

Croatia actually did enact a Sunday law, but that's Croatia, not the United States, and according to the Adventist understanding of the prophecy, it's the *American Congress,* not the European Parliament, that will violate every principle of its Constitution by enacting a Sunday law.[21] I'm more likely to believe we're seeing a prophetic fulfillment when Sunday law proposals start to make waves in the United States Congress.

Having stated this caution, I will also say that I do see what has been going on in Europe as significant to our understanding of prophecy. The Roman Catholic Church was extremely influential in the enactment of the Croatian Sunday law, and it gave strong support to the effort to insert a work-free-Sunday clause into the European Working Time Directive. This, together with John Paul II's *Dies Domini* urging legal protection of Sunday as a day of rest and worship, tells me that the Roman Catholic Church would give its full support to any Sunday legislation proposed to the United States Congress. I believe that will happen someday, and when it does, we'll be justified in thinking the final crisis is drawing near.

Chapter 12 of this book is titled "Expectations." In it, I pointed out that the Jews living at Christ's time had false concepts regarding what the Messiah would do, and this led them to misunderstand Christ's work and to reject Him. I concluded chapter 12 by suggesting that Adventists also face the danger of being misled by false concepts. And unfortunately, people who misunderstand end-time events will be tempted go some other direction than where God is leading.

Throughout her career as a prophet, Ellen White warned that Sunday legislation passed by the United States Congress in violation of the Sabbath of the fourth commandment will be *the primary moral issue* in the final conflict. Thus, no sign of the end is more likely to arouse Adventist expectations about the end time than Sunday laws. However, we must be very careful about jumping to the conclusion that every hint of a Sunday law, whether it's in Podunkville, Israel, Croatia, or the European Union, is a sign that the final crisis is imminent. In my opinion, major alarms about Sunday laws anywhere other than in the United States Congress put a faulty prophetic interpretation on a current event, and that can be spiritually dangerous in that it can lead to extremism and fanaticism. You may be able to handle a bit of misguided prophetic interpretation without becoming fanatical. The person you share it with may not.

1. Joseph Bates, *The Seventh-day Sabbath, a Perpetual Sign, From the Beginning to the Entering Into the Gates of the Holy City, According to the Commandment* (New Bedford, MA: Press of Benjamin Lindsey, 1847), 59.

2. James and Ellen White, *A Word to the Little Flock,* facsimile ed. (Washington, DC: Review and Herald®, n.d.), 19. This is text from the first edition of the *Little Flock* book, which Ellen White later removed.

3. See White, *The Great Controversy,* 433–450, 582–592, 624.

4. http://en.wikipedia.org/wiki/McGowan_v._Maryland.

5. http://www.vatican.va/holy_father/john_paul_ii/apost_letters/documents/hf_jp-ii _apl_05071998_dies-domini_en.html

6. *Dies Domini,* chap. 4:66, 67.

7. Vatican Radio, "The Family: Work and Rest: Pope Issues Letter Urging Balance in Family Life," *Catholic Online,* September 28, 2010, http://catholic.org/hf/family /story.php?id-38458.

8. Gil Hoffman, "Netanyahu to Decide Fate of 5-Day Work Week in Fall," *Jerusalem Post,* July 4, 2011, http://www.jpost.com/DiplomacyAndPolitics/Article.aspx?id=227887.

9. "Together for Decent Working Hours!" European Sunday Alliance, http://www .europeanstudayalliance.eu/site/home/article/74.html.

10. "High Court Reaffirms Ban on Sunday Shopping," *Deutsche Welle*, February 12, 2009, http://www.dw-world.de/dw/article/0,,4953600,00.html.

11. Megan Brauner, "Croatia: Parliament Limits Sunday Shopping," Adventist News Network, September 23, 2008, http://news.adventist.org/2008/09.

12. Brighton G. Kavaloh, "European Sunday Weekly Rest Day Legislation Remains Unlawful," unpublished report, http://www.adventreligio-legal-perspective .org/kavalohoneuropeanrestlaw.pdf.

13. Ibid.

14. European Commission, "Working Time Directive," http://ec.europa.eu/social /main.jsp?catId=706&langLd=en&intPageId=205.

15. European Commission, "Written Declaration," February 2, 2009, http://www .europarl.europa.eu/sides/getDoc.do?pubRef=-//EP//NONSGML+WDECL+P6 -DCL-2009-0009+0+DOC+PDF+V0//EN&language=EN.

16. "List of the Organisations Which Supported the First European Conference for the Protection of a Work-free Sunday," Keep Sunday Special, http://www.keepsundayspecial .org.uk/Web/Content/Default.aspx?Content=79.

17. "According to EU Law, Sunday Is the Weekly Rest Day," February 21, 2009, http://www.presentruth.com/2009/02/according-to-eu-law-sunday-is-the-weekly-rest -day.

18. "Why Sunday Should Be Included as a Weekly Rest Day in the Revised Working Time Directive," press release, http://csc.ceceurope.org/fileadmin/filer/csc/Social _Economic_Issues/CSCProtectionofSunday_EN.pdf.

19. "The EU Must Keep Sunday, Says Catholic Church," theTRUMPET.com, November 18, 2008, http://www.ktfministry.org/news/393/european-bishops-still-pressing-for -sunday-rest.

20. "European Bishops Still Pressing for Sunday Rest," February 23, 2009, Keep the Faith, http://www.ktfministry.org/news/393/european-bishops-still-pressing-for-sunday-rest.

21. See White, *Testimonies,* 5:451.

ADDENDUM:

Religion and Sunday Rest Laws

In an article in *Liberty* magazine analyzing the current secular support for Sunday legislation, Edwin Cook said,

> Sunday laws make up a large part of American religious and legal history. In the secularized environment of a highly pluralistic society, Sunday-rest advocates may appeal to a more general argument of societal well-being divorced from religious connotations to support Sunday legislation. However, if Sunday laws should ever be enforced in America, either at the state or national level, sufficient evidence exists that reveals the implicit religious foundations upon which such arguments are grounded.
>
> No matter how persuasively its advocates present their case, the centuries-long religiously interwoven history of Sunday-rest laws shows their true character. By virtue of the immense difficulty of distinguishing between a day of rest for worship (religious motivation) and a day of rest for recuperation (sociological/physiological motivation), it is indeed evident that religious groups can argue the latter in order to achieve the former. This reason alone is sufficient grounds to argue against Sunday-rest laws from a historical perspective.[1]

1. Edwin Cook, "The Rest of the Story," *Liberty,* March/April 2011, 29. At the time Cook wrote this article, he was completing a doctoral degree in church-state relations at Baylor University in Waco, Texas.

CHAPTER 15

A Dangerous Expectation: Sinless Perfection

I think I'm safe in saying that most conservative Protestant Christians believe it's important to accept Jesus during this present lifetime, because when we die, our eternal destinies are sealed. There will be no opportunities to switch loyalties from Satan to Christ after our deaths.

But now think of this: according to the Bible, some people will live to see Jesus come. John said that at Christ's second coming the wicked will call for the rocks and the mountains to fall on them (Revelation 6:16). Jesus said, presumably of the wicked, that at His coming "all the peoples of the earth will mourn" (Matthew 24:30). And Paul said that God's people "will not all sleep" (1 Corinthians 15:51); those who live to see Jesus come will instead be caught up with the resurrected saints to "meet the Lord in the air. And so we will be with the Lord forever" (1 Thessalonians 4:17).

So, when will those who live to see Jesus come have their last opportunities to accept Him? Most Christians would probably point to the Second Coming, but Seventh-day Adventists have a unique response to that question. We say that opportunity will end shortly *before* Christ returns. I went into some detail about the biblical basis for this conclusion in my book *How to Think About the End Time*,[1] so I'll give only a summary here.

Jesus gave parables about the separation of the righteous from the wicked at the end of time: the wheat and the tares, the good and the bad fish, the wise and the foolish virgins, and the sheep and the goats (see Matthew 13:36–43, 47–50; 25:1–13, 31–46). All of this suggests that the separation of God's people from the wicked will occur *at* Christ's second coming. However, Revelation provides an important additional insight. It identifies the same two groups: the righteous, who receive the seal of God, and the wicked, who receive the mark of the beast (see Revelation 7:1–4; 14:1–5; 13:16, 17). But notice that according to Revelation 16:1, 2, the first plague will be poured out on those who receive the mark of the beast. Obviously, this means that it will have been decided by this time who will receive the mark of the beast—and who will receive the seal of God. And since the seven last plagues will fall on the earth *before* Christ's return, it is evident that everyone alive will have made their final decision either for or against Christ *prior* to His return. Jesus' parables are correct in stating that the *physical* separation of the righteous from the wicked will occur *at* His second coming, but obviously, whether a person is saved or lost must be determined *before* He returns. Therefore, the opportunity to switch sides in the conflict between good and evil will have to end *before* Jesus comes. Adventists call this termination of the opportunity to accept Jesus as Savior "the close of probation."

No Mediator after the close of probation

Adventists add one other detail to this scenario. Ellen White has stated very clearly that there will be no Mediator in the heavenly sanctuary after the close of probation. She said, "An angel returning from earth announces that his work is done; the final test has been brought upon the world, and all who have proved themselves loyal to the divine precepts have received 'the seal of the living God.' Then Jesus ceases His intercession in the sanctuary above."[2] And, a few sentences later, she wrote that "when [Jesus] leaves the sanctuary, darkness covers the inhabitants of the earth. In that fearful time the righteous must live in the sight of a holy God without an intercessor."[3]

The reason for this conclusion is obvious: once everyone who is going to accept Jesus has done so, and once all those who are going to reject

Him have done so, there will be no more need of a Mediator's efforts to save human beings from sin. However, all the other functions of Christ's mediatorial ministry will still be available to His people after the close of probation, as I will show in a moment.

Ellen White elaborated further on the ending of this aspect of Jesus' mediatorial ministry in two other statements in *The Great Controversy*. She said,

> Those who are living upon the earth when the intercession of Christ shall cease in the sanctuary above are to stand in the sight of a holy God without a mediator. Their robes must be spotless, their characters must be purified from sin by the blood of sprinkling. Through the grace of God and their own diligent effort they must be conquerors in the battle with evil. While the investigative judgment is going forward in heaven, while the sins of penitent believers are being removed from the sanctuary, there is to be a special work of purification, of putting away of sin, among God's people upon earth.[4]

> Now, while our great High Priest is making the atonement for us, we should seek to become perfect in Christ. Not even by a thought could our Saviour be brought to yield to the power of temptation. Satan finds in human hearts some point where he can gain a foothold; some sinful desire is cherished, by means of which his temptations assert their power. But Christ declared of Himself: "The prince of this world cometh, and hath nothing in Me." John 14:30. Satan could find nothing in the Son of God that would enable him to gain the victory. He had kept His Father's commandments, and there was no sin in Him that Satan could use to his advantage. This is the condition in which those must be found who shall stand in the time of trouble.[5]

The implications of these statements are ominous. They suggest that God's people must become perfect—able to live without sinning—before probation closes. If they can't, they'll lose their eternal lives. Unfortunately, this idea has made some Adventists extremely anxious, so it's important that we understand (1) what it will mean to live without a Mediator after the close of probation, and (2) the state God's people must reach in order to survive spiritually during that time.

Living without a Mediator

Before we can answer the question about what it will be like to live *without* a Mediator after the close of probation, we first must inquire what it means to live *with* a Mediator today. What is Jesus, in His role as Mediator, doing for us right now?

In my book *How to Think About the End Time,* I identified seven things that Jesus is doing for us as our Mediator.

1. Through the Holy Spirit, He draws the unconverted to Himself.
2. Through the Spirit, He dwells in the minds and hearts of His people.
3. He forgives us of the sins we repent of and confess.
4. He covers us with the robe of His righteousness.
5. He gives us the power to overcome sin.
6. He responds to our prayers.
7. He defends us against Satan's accusations.

Which of these seven aspects of Jesus' mediatorial ministry will be available to God's people after the close of probation?

1. Will He continue to draw the unconverted to Himself? *No.*
2. Will He still dwell in the minds of His people through the Holy Spirit? *Yes!*
3. Will He forgive us of the sins we repent of and confess? *If we won't sin after the close of probation, we won't need forgiveness for sin.*
4. Will He cover us with the robe of His righteousness? *Yes!*
5. Will He give us the power to overcome sin? *Yes!*

6. Will He respond to our prayers? *Yes!*

7. Will He defend us against Satan's accusations? *Yes!*

Of the seven aspects of Christ's mediatorial ministry that I mentioned, five will still be available to us *after* the close of probation, and we won't need the other two.* It's true that Jesus will no longer be our Mediator after the close of probation, but He will continue to bless us with everything we need then that we receive through His mediatorial ministry today. Therefore, we need not be afraid of living without a Mediator.

How perfect must we be?

The question still remains, How perfect must we be after the close of probation? A few pages back, we noted that Ellen White said our "robes must be spotless, [our] characters must be purified from sin by the blood of sprinkling." She said that "not even by a thought could our Saviour be brought to yield to the power of temptation. . . . He had kept His Father's commandments, and there was no sin in Him that Satan could use to his advantage." Then came these ominous words: "This is the condition in which those must be found who shall stand in the time of trouble."

Some Adventists insist that we must be absolutely sinless in order to live without a Mediator after the close of probation. This conclusion is based on the supposition that since forgiveness of sin won't be available after the close of probation, we must reach a condition of absolute sinless perfection *before* the close of probation so that we *won't* sin—indeed, *can't* sin—*after* the close of probation. This, I believe, is one of the unhealthy expectations that some Adventists have drawn from our theology of the end time and the close of probation.

Please understand this: *It's possible that absolute perfection of character will be God's requirement for those who must live without a Mediator after*

---

* I believe that God's people won't knowingly sin after the close of probation. However, in my book *How to Think About the End Time,* I point out significant evidence that we will still have character defects after the close of probation, and these may cause us to say or do things that God would tell us we shouldn't say or do (see pages 148, 175, 176). I believe that forgiveness for such "sins" will still be available.

the close of probation. I don't know for sure whether or not that's the case. What I do know is that an insistence on absolute perfection is damaging to our mental and spiritual health and decreases rather than increases how prepared we are for the end time.

Understanding the following three kinds of spiritual perfection may help us determine what kind of perfection will be required of us after the close of probation:

1. *There's the perfection we have when Christ's righteousness covers us.* Of this kind of perfection, Ellen White said, "Christ's character stands in place of your character, and you are accepted before God just as if you had not sinned."[6] Those who are covered with Christ's righteousness may still have many character defects, but because Christ's righteousness covers them, God counts them as perfect in the sense of being sinless.

2. *There's the perfection that is maturity of Christian character.* Mature Christians aren't necessarily sinless. But while they may sin occasionally, they don't sin carelessly and continually.*

3. *There's perfection as living completely without sin—never sinning.* Once Christians reach absolute sinless perfection, they won't sin, nor will they need forgiveness for sin.

I believe that God's people will need the covering of Christ's righteousness throughout the time of trouble after the close of probation. I also believe that those who pass through that difficult time will have developed mature Christian characters. I think the major issue is whether we must be totally and absolutely sinless. There are several aspects to my response to this question.

First, even if God does require absolute sinless perfection of His people who live after the close of probation, they cannot claim it. John said, "If we claim to be without sin, we deceive ourselves and the truth is not in us" (1 John 1:8).

---

* Compare the following texts in the King James Version with the same texts in the New International Version: Philippians 3:15; Ephesians 4:12, 23.

Second, even if God plans to require absolute sinless perfection after the close of probation, we don't understand enough about the working of our minds to recognize when we have achieved it. If we knew we had it, we could claim it, at least in our own minds.

Third, the One who will know when we have achieved absolute sinless perfection is Christ.

Fourth, our task is not to worry about how perfect we are or how perfect we must become. If we focus on these things, we'll live in a continual state of anxiety about whether or not God has accepted us. We need to recognize that Christ counts us as perfect today, even though we still have many character defects that cause us to do and say some wrong things.

Fifth, our task is to cooperate with Christ in dealing with the sins that He reveals to us today and let Him be the One to decide when we're ready for the close of probation. I can assure you that if you are sincerely claiming His righteousness each day and doing your best to live His life, He won't close probation's door until you are ready for it to be closed.

One of the best comments I've ever read about Christian perfection was made some four hundred years ago by the Dutch theologian Jacobus Arminius (1560–1609).* He said,

> While I never asserted that a believer could perfectly keep the precepts of Christ in this life, I never denied it, but always left it as a matter which has still to be decided. I think the time may be far more happily and usefully employed in prayers to obtain what is lacking in each of us, and in serious admonitions that every one endeavor to proceed and press forward towards the mark of perfection, than when spent in such disputations.[7]

---

* Arminius is famous today for the branch of Protestant theology that he inspired. Arminianism proposes that human beings have a free will in matters of salvation. That stands in contrast to Calvinistic theology, which proposes that everyone's eternal fate is a matter of God's choice rather than the choice of the individual. Arminianism is not in any way related to the ethnic Armenians (note the difference in spelling) and their brand of Orthodox Christianity.

Let me assure you that if God sees that you must be absolutely, sinlessly perfect in order to live without a Mediator after the close of probation, then as long as you are cooperating with Him each day in your character development, He will get you there. You won't know when you've achieved it, but He will, and that's all that matters. So stop worrying about it!

The final generation

E. J. Waggoner and A. T. Jones made quite an issue of the perfection that God's end-time saints would need in order to live after the close of probation without a Mediator. M. L. Andreasen, a prominent Adventist theologian in the 1930s and 1940s, developed this concept into a detailed "final generation" theology, which proposed that one of the reasons why God's people will need sinless perfection after the close of probation is that by their perfect obedience they will complete the plan of salvation. He expounded at length on this idea in chapter 20 of his book *The Sanctuary Service*.[8]

As Andreasen understood it, God has been waiting six thousand years for the development of a community of saints who can demonstrate to the universe that His law can be kept by the very weakest human being, and He will finally achieve that objective in the final generation. Andreasen adamantly insisted that God's people *must* demonstrate this before Jesus can return, because should they not, Satan would be proven correct in his claim that God's law cannot be kept, and he would emerge victorious in the great controversy. Andreasen believed that God is fitting up a people—the 144,000—to be sinlessly perfect ambassadors for Him during the time of trouble, and by living perfect lives during the most intense distress the world has ever known, they will prove that God's law *can* be kept. Thus, they will disprove Satan's claim, thereby defeating him and vindicating God. And when they've provided this demonstration, Jesus can come. The opening paragraph of the chapter titled "The Last Generation" in *The Sanctuary Service* introduces this view:

The final demonstration of what the gospel can do in and for humanity is still in the future. Christ showed the way. He took a human body, and in that body demonstrated the power of God. Men are to follow His example and prove that what God did in Christ, He can do in every human being who submits to Him. The world is awaiting this demonstration. (Rom. 8:19.) When it has been accomplished, the end will come. God will have fulfilled His plan. He will have shown Himself true and Satan a liar. His government will stand vindicated.[9]

Andreasen also said that it is up to the final generation to defeat Satan:

In the last generation [of saints] God is vindicated and *Satan defeated.*[10]

[Satan] had failed in his conflict with Christ, but he might yet succeed with men. So he went to "make war with the remnant of her seed, which keep the commandments of God, and have the testimony of Jesus Christ." Rev. 12:17. *If he could overcome them he might not be defeated.*[11]

Through the last generation of saints God stands finally vindicated. *Through them He defeats Satan and wins His case.* They form a vital part of the plan of God.[12]

I have a *major* problem with the idea that God won't have defeated Satan until the final generation demonstrates their loyalty to His law, because it puts the responsibility for the completion of the plan of salvation on sinful human beings, and that simply cannot be! *Jesus defeated Satan by His life and His death!* John proclaimed, "Now have come the salvation and the power and the kingdom of our God, and the authority of his Messiah. For the accuser of our brothers, who accuses them before our God day and night, *has been hurled down*" (Revelation 12:10; emphasis added). *Jesus* demonstrated Satan's claims to be false. *Jesus'* perfect life and death defeated Satan once and for all; God doesn't need the final generation to defeat Satan again. *Jesus* demonstrated that God's law can be kept, and once *He* made that demonstration, the battle was won. I have no doubt that the entire universe will be watching the response of the saints during the final crisis and that there will be ways in which we will vindicate God, but this won't be in any sense an essential part of the plan of salvation that would be left incomplete should we fail to do our part to vindicate God.

Conclusion

At the time of Christ's first coming, the Jews held some false ideas about what His mission was, which led them to develop some very warped and spiritually dangerous expectations. We who live just prior to Jesus' second coming need to view their mistake as a warning, for we are in just as much danger of adopting dangerous expectations about the end time. One of these dangerous expectations is that we must be absolutely sinless after the close of probation. Please note carefully what I said, and especially what I did *not* say. I did *not* say that the expectation that God's people will attain sinless perfection after the close of probation is *false*. It may be that God will bring us to the point of sinless perfection as a preparation for living without a Mediator after the close of probation. What I *am* saying is that for the reasons I've shared with you in this chapter, to *expect* this and to claim that it is a goal that people must reach is to turn it into a *dangerous* expectation. And the spiritual results of this expectation can be just as detrimental as were the warped expectations of the Jews two thousand years ago, for it leads us to forget that our perfection will always reside in Christ, not within ourselves. We need to trust in His righteousness, do our best to follow His lead in our character development, and *let Him decide when we are "good enough" to live without a Mediator after the close of probation.*

---

1. Marvin Moore, *How to Think About the End Time* (Nampa, ID: Pacific Press®, 2001), 144–146.

2. White, *The Great Controversy*, 613.

3. Ibid., 614.

4. Ibid., 425.

5. Ibid., 623.

6. Ellen G. White, *Steps to Christ* (Washington, DC: Review and Herald®, 1956), 62.

7. Cited by Woodrow Whidden in "Grace, Free Will, and Judgment," *Adventist Review,* October 14, 2010, 19.

8. M. L. Andreasen, *The Sanctuary Service* (Washington, DC: Review and Herald®, 1947).

9. Ibid., 299.

10. Ibid., 303, 304; emphasis added.

11. Ibid., 310; emphasis added.

12. Ibid., 319; emphasis added.

PART 4

Using Our Time Wisely During the Delay

CHAPTER 16

The Latter Rain: Revival

In his book *Revive Us Again,* Mark Finley said, "The second coming of Christ may seem to be delayed, but our preparation for His return should never be delayed."[1] Two of the end-time themes that Ellen White considered particularly important are what she called "the latter rain" and "the loud cry." In this chapter and the next, I will discuss the latter rain and the preparation we must make in order to receive it—reformation and the revival that precedes and motivates it. I will discuss the loud cry in chapter 18.

Ellen White described two kinds of spiritual "rain"—what she called "the former rain" and "the latter rain." She used these terms as metaphors of the work of the Holy Spirit in the lives of individuals and, corporately, of the body of Christ, the church. In the case of individuals, *the former rain* refers to the early stages of the Holy Spirit's work on the mind and heart, which begins when a person accepts Jesus and experiences conversion. Believers must allow the Holy Spirit to continue His work within them throughout the remainder of their lives. In its corporate sense, the term *the former rain* refers to the outpouring of the Holy Spirit on the apostles on the Day of Pentecost, which enabled them to proclaim the meaning of Christ's death and resurrection with such power that three thousand people were baptized that same day (Acts 2:41).*

The latter rain can also be thought of in individual and corporate senses. In the individual sense, Ellen White said that the latter rain "represents the completion of the work of God's grace in the soul."[2] For Adventists who are concerned about end-time perfection, I propose that the latter rain will give the finishing touch to those who have been actively engaged in developing their character up to that point. In the corporate sense, the latter rain refers to a powerful outpouring of the Holy Spirit upon the church as a whole that will enable God's people to proclaim the final warning to the world with a power that is similar to that with which the apostles proclaimed the message of Christ's death and resurrection at Pentecost.

While we can distinguish between the individual and corporate aspects of the former and latter rains, they actually go together. The latter rain will fall upon God's people corporately only when they become serious about revival and reformation individually. Thus, it's critical that we understand the meaning of revival and reformation. Even more important, we each must incorporate these experiences into our own lives. Revival and reformation are twin experiences. Reformation must follow revival; if it doesn't, the revival wasn't genuine.

Revival means an invigoration of the spiritual life. A group of people can be revived only as the individuals in that group experience a renewing of their spiritual lives. Revival begins with an intensified devotional life, especially prayer, Bible study, and fellowship. These of course take time, which is one of the major reasons why so many of us don't experience revival. We fill our lives so full that we find it easy to let entire days slip by without cultivating our spiritual lives. We keep saying, "I'll do it tomorrow," but tomorrow's pressures are just as intense as today's, and "tomorrow" slips by in the same way "today" did.

I know you've already heard it many times, but it's really true that we can't just *take* the time; we have to *make* the time. Another way of saying

---

* Later, five thousand men accepted the apostles' message and became Christians (Acts 4:4), and since it is likely that in most cases, their wives and children would also have become Christians with them, the total was probably more like fifteen or twenty thousand.

it is that we must make Bible study, prayer, and fellowship a priority in our lives. If we don't, other things will invariably take over. The devil, of course, knows this, and he invents a thousand ways to keep our minds busy so that we don't have—or don't *think* we have—time to spend with God.

Righteousness by faith

The beginning point for revival is the gospel of righteousness by faith. If we don't understand righteousness by faith, we are in great danger of falling into either legalism or cheap grace. Righteousness by faith consists of two parts: justification and sanctification. Justification is associated with revival, so we'll take a look at it now. Sanctification belongs with reformation, so we'll consider it in the next chapter.

I presented a detailed examination of the biblical basis for justification in my book *Forever His,*[3] which is my commentary on Romans 1–8. I also discussed justification as presented in both the Bible and Ellen White's writings in section 1 of my book *Conquering the Dragon Within.*[4] I'll give just a summary here.

I have a very loving relationship with my wife, Lois. She's the dearest friend I have ever had or hope to have. We converse easily. I have discussed with her some of the deepest secrets of my heart, including my failures. She accepts me just as I am and keeps on loving me. What if Lois didn't do that? What if she reminded me every day about my failures? What if our relationship depended on my being perfect and never doing anything that disappointed her? That, unfortunately, is how some people view their relationship with God. Some of them think that unless they obey God perfectly, He won't accept them. Others think they must be absolutely perfect in order to live without a Mediator after the close of probation. Those who hold this second variety of perfectionism may accept their imperfections today, but their focus is still on perfection.

Having said this, I will point out that it's true that God will only take perfect people into heaven. If we have one sin in our lives, one defect in our characters, we're out! However, the God who created us also loves us deeply, and He *wants* us to be in heaven with Him. So He has a problem:

He wants us in heaven, but we're sinful human beings, so He can't let us in. That's a pretty difficult problem to solve! If it were up to me to figure out how to get sinners into heaven, you and I would be in deep trouble. Fortunately, God is a lot wiser than I am, and He's come up with a way to count us as perfect so He can allow us into heaven even though we're quite imperfect.

Romans 3:20 explains how it works. Paul said, "No one will be declared righteous in his sight by observing the law; rather, through the law we become conscious of sin." It doesn't matter how "good" we've been; nothing we do can earn us His acceptance.

So, on what basis does God accept us? Verse 21 answers the question: "But now apart from the law the righteousness *of God* has been made known" (empasis added). Paul means that God provides for you and me a righteousness that doesn't depend on how well we've kept His laws. He stated this idea even more clearly in Philippians: "I consider [all things] garbage, that I may gain Christ and be found in him, not having a righteousness of my own that comes from [keeping] the law, but that which is through faith in Christ—*the righteousness that comes from God* on the basis of faith" (Philippians 3:8, 9; empasis added).

Notice that in both Philippians and Romans, Paul spoke of a righteousness *from God* that is apart from law—that is, apart from all our efforts to keep the law. Paul's point is that since we can never work hard enough to gain the righteousness we need in order to be perfect, God gives us *His* righteousness. Once God's righteousness* becomes our righteousness, we are perfect in His sight. Ellen White stated it succinctly: "Christ's character stands in place of your character, and you are accepted before God just as if you had not sinned."[5] *God's accepting you and me just as if we had not sinned means that God counts us as perfect even though we still have the moral defects that have caused us to sin previously and that will cause us to sin again!*

I typically give eight or ten weekend seminars every year in churches around North America. Most of the time, at least two of my presentations are on righteousness by faith. Often I will ask everyone in the

* God's righteousness and Christ's righteousness are the same thing.

congregation who is perfect to please raise their hands. One or two tim-id souls may inch their hands slightly above their heads, but most people keep their hands firmly in their laps. Then I ask everyone to raise a hand. Usually, I have to say it two or three times before everyone has a hand in the air. When most of the congregation has raised a hand, I say, "Now I'm looking at all the perfect people here today!" which usually brings a chuckle. Then I say, "None of us is perfect within ourselves, but if we have accepted Christ as our Savior, then His 'character stands in place of [our] character, and [we] are accepted before God *just as if [we] had not sinned.*' "

Have you been struggling to be perfect, to overcome every sin in your life? God is very pleased with that desire. I'm sure He appreciates every effort you've put forth to reach that objective, and He wants you to keep on doing your best. However, I must hasten to add two qualifications to that statement. First, you can't do it alone. I think most Christians are aware of that. They know that if they're to overcome their temptations, they must have the power of the Holy Spirit. But when they slip and fall, they think they've failed. Some even think they must not have had a re-lationship with Jesus after all, because if they had, they wouldn't have sinned.

This brings me to the second qualification: We don't lose our rela-tionship with Jesus just because we sinned. I've never read a more clear explanation of this thought than the one I found in a statement by Ellen White: "When it is in the heart to obey God, when efforts are put forth to this end, Jesus accepts this disposition and effort as man's best service, and He makes up for the deficiency with His own divine merit."[6]

Please note: "When it is in the heart to obey God" means we *want* to obey Him. "When efforts are put forth to this end" means we're *doing our very best* to obey Him. When that is the case, we don't have to feel that God rejects us or that we've lost our relationship with Jesus. To the contrary, Jesus *immediately* applies His divine merit to our failure, and we continue to be "accepted by God just as if you had not sinned."

There's one other aspect to justification that we must discuss: We re-ceive it "by faith." When Paul told the Philippians that he had a "righteousness that comes *from* God," he added that it comes from God *by faith.* (See also Romans 3:20–22.) God doesn't demand that we be perfect before He will accept us, but He does ask us to *believe* that He accepts us and covers us with Christ's righteousness. This is particularly hard for people to do when they feel overwhelmed by guilt for the sins they've just committed. We should by all means confess the sins; but in addition to confessing, we should thank God that He accepts us in spite of what we just did or said. I don't hesitate to say that those who continually wallow in guilt over their sins will not overcome them. We must *believe* that God forgives us and accepts us right where we are.

Some Christians tend to think that they should be further along in their Christian experience than they are at the moment. But God doesn't think that way. Wherever we are in our walk with Him, He says, "That's OK. Now let's move forward from here." God is aware, of course, that we could have been further along in our Christian experience had we made different choices. But He doesn't throw that up to us. He's glad we're turning to Him *now.* Each day, each hour, is a new starting point with God, so we should praise Him for His forgiveness and ask Him to help us be more successful in overcoming that besetting sin the next time we're tempted.

That's justification, and it's the beginning point for revival. There are three other essentials for experiencing revival: Bible study, prayer, and Christian fellowship.

Bible study

When I study the Bible, I like to begin by bowing my head and asking God to help me to find and hear what the text I'm about to read has to say to me and my life today. It might be some aspect of character development, the wisdom I need to deal with a problem in my life, or simply to understand God better. Some days I come up rather dry, but I don't worry about that because I know that on other days my Bible study will yield some very meaningful insights.

There are a number of good ways to study the Bible. One is to *just read it.* A person can start with Genesis and read through to Revelation.

While this is a useful method of Bible study for anyone, I especially recommend it for those who know little or nothing about the Bible. Reading it through will give you a sense—a "feel"—for the various parts of the Bible: history, poetry, prophecy, Gospels, apostolic letters, and so on. If you're already quite familiar with the Bible as a whole, you might wish to read just one of its books. For several weeks, I've been reading through all four Gospels; I'm about a third of the way through John.

Another way to study the Bible is with a prepared study guide. There are many; one of the best is the adult Sabbath School Quarterly, published by the General Conference Sabbath School Department. There's a lesson for each day of the entire three-month period—the quarter. The church also publishes quarterlies for the various age groups preceding the adults: kindergarten, primary, junior, early teen, teen, and young adult. Most churches distribute these quarterlies at the beginning of each quarter, with the cost being covered by the Sabbath School expense offering that typically is taken at the beginning of the class period.*

A third way to study the Bible is by topic. This is especially helpful if you're struggling with a particular issue, such as money, envy, justification, love, and so on. In some cases, you may find a book or study guide on that topic at an Adventist Book Center or at another store that sells religious books and other materials. Or you can use a Bible concordance to trace a particular word through the Bible. You'll learn a lot about that word and about the Bible too. Good Bible software is also a very useful tool for doing topical Bible studies. I use a program called "BibleWorks."†
And I recommend that you invest in a good Bible commentary and Bible dictionary. *The Seventh-day Adventist Bible Commentary* covers all the books of the Bible in seven volumes. The entire set, which includes a Bible dictionary and more, is available from any Adventist Book Center and from the Web site www.adventistbookcenter.com.

I also recommend that you spend time studying the biblical basis for

---

* I encourage you to give at least one dollar per week to the Sabbath School Expense Offering. This will easily cover the cost of your quarterly plus help purchase the children's quarterlies and Sabbath School magazines.

† See http://www.bibleworks.com.

the doctrines of the Seventh-day Adventist Church. A number of excellent books are available to guide you through this study, including *Bible Readings for the Home*,[7] the *Handbook of Seventh-day Adventist Theology*,[8] and *Seventh-day Adventists Believe*.[9] These books are also available through the Adventist Book Center. This study will help to ground you in the basic teachings of the Bible, thus building your confidence in your Christian walk.

However you choose to study your Bible—and you'll probably use all of these methods eventually—it's important that you make the time to just *do it*.

Prayer

There is no revival without prayer. Ellen White said, "A revival of true godliness among us is the greatest and most urgent of all our needs, . . . [and it] need be expected only in answer to prayer."[10]

We don't have to use any kind of holy language to talk to God. I much prefer addressing God as "You" rather than as "Thee" and "Thou." Spanish Christians typically pray to God using the familiar second-person pronoun *Tu* rather than the more formal *Usted*.

Some people wonder *how* to pray. When Jesus' disciples asked Him about that, He gave them what has come to be known as the Lord's Prayer (Luke 11:1–4; see also Matthew 6:9–13). One of the things that has impressed me most about that prayer is its simplicity. It's short; there's no flowery language; and it isn't complicated. Suppose you were sharing your concerns with your best friend. That's how you talk to God. Ellen White said, "Prayer is the opening of the heart to God as to a friend."[11]

If we are to be prepared for the final events of the future, it's imperative that we pray regularly *now*. Regardless of how busy we may be, we must set aside the time to talk to God every day. If you haven't been praying regularly, you may find it helpful to begin with just five or ten minutes and gradually increase that time to twenty or thirty minutes or longer.

You can also pause for a moment here and there throughout the day for a miniconversation with God. I think that's what Paul meant when he said that we should "pray without ceasing" (1 Thessalonians 5:17, NKJV). Don't be rigid about the time. It goes without saying that you'll have more time for prayer on some days than you do on others.

If you commute to work, try using that time to talk to God. After all, when you have a friend or loved one with you, you can talk to them as you maneuver through traffic, can't you? You can do the same thing when you talk to God while you're driving. Of course, you'll have to keep your eye on the road and watch for traffic lights and stop signs. But God understands that. He's just glad that you're talking to Him!

I like to begin my prayer time with praise and adoration. Often, I bring into my imagination an image of the universe as photographed by the Hubble Space Telescope. Astronomers have discovered that there are millions of galaxies in the universe, and I am frankly awed to think that my God created all of that! I'm even more awed to think that the God who created the vastness of this universe wants to talk to *me*—little old *me*—here on planet Earth. So, I praise God for His mighty power and the privilege of addressing Him as *my Friend*!

I'm accustomed to praying to God the Father and closing with "in Jesus' name," but I'm learning to address Jesus and the Holy Spirit in my prayers too. Some days I'll spend my entire prayer time talking to the Father, then the next day pray to the Son, and the following day to the Holy Spirit. Sometimes I slip back into praying to the Father, and there's no harm in that, but when I notice it, I go back to praying to the Son or the Holy Spirit.

What should we pray about? Most anything that concerns us. Here's a short list:

- Ask God to give you the wisdom to deal appropriately with whatever problems you're facing.
- Talk to Him about the people who are closest to you. Thank Him for those who love you, and ask Him to give you the patience to get along with those you're in conflict with.
- Ask God to continue working with the hearts of your friends and loved ones who aren't following Jesus.

- Ask Him to show you the defects of character you need to correct in order to be the happiest and most effective Christian you can be.
- Ask Him to give you the wisdom to take advantage of opportunities to share Jesus and His love with others.
- Pray for the leaders of the church: your pastor and your local conference, union, and General Conference officials. Also pray for government leaders.
- Confess your sins and character defects, and ask God to give you the wisdom and power to overcome them.

What can you expect to have happen when you pray? Most of the time, nothing spectacular. You'll experience times when you feel very close to God. Those are the times to cherish and to seek to repeat. They will most likely come to you more frequently as you become experienced at praying. However, I caution people not to *expect* some overwhelming feeling. The fact that you don't feel anything unusual doesn't mean that your prayers are not meaningful and effective.

One further comment about the devotional life: There have been occasions when I've had the time for Bible study and prayer, but something inside of me wanted to get on with the other things on my agenda. On further reflection, I realized I needed to make my devotional life more a "have to" than a "want to." I didn't have a yearning to spend time with God. While the psalmist sang, "Oh, how I love your law" (Psalm 119:97), that wasn't my experience. So I started praying, "God, please change my attitude. Help me to come to the place where I long to spend time with You."

Then one day I read once again Jesus' beatitude, "Blessed are those who hunger and thirst for righteousness, for they will be filled" (Matthew 5:6). As I reflected on those words, I realized that even though I didn't always feel a great longing to spend time with God, I recognized the problem and wanted to change. That in itself is a hungering and thirsting after righteousness. So now I keep praying that God will help me come to the place where I cherish my devotional times and no longer feel the urge to get on with other things. I'm not there yet, and I suppose that there will always be times when the busyness of life will press on my mind. But I keep resisting that feeling and growing in my appreciation for the times that I do spend with God. Ellen White counseled us to "educate [our] mind[s] to love the Bible, love the prayer meeting, to love the hour of meditation, and above all, the hour when the soul communes with God."[12] I'm trying to do that.

Fellowship

Another element of revival is fellowship with other Christians. Sabbath School and the church worship service especially come to mind, as do midweek prayer meetings. Association with other Christians one-on-one and in small groups are very helpful forms of fellowship. Some people like to meet as a small group once a week. For several years, my wife, Lois, and I have been meeting that way with a Baptist couple who are about our age. We don't mind skipping a week here and there when one of us is out of town or has to attend a church function, but we always get back together the next week for an evening meal and Bible study. These times have become very meaningful to all of us.

There have been a few occasions in my life when I felt especially close to God during a worship service. I remember attending the early morning Sabbath worship service at the Union College church during the alumni weekend that marked forty years since I graduated. I don't know why, but I felt an overwhelming sense of awe as the congregation sang the opening hymn. In fact, I found the entire service so moving that at the close, when my wife and some other friends left, I stayed behind for the second service. My heart was touched in the same way on the second Sabbath of the General Conference Session in Atlanta, Georgia, in 2010. The congregation stood to sing "We Have This Hope," and partway through the song I choked up and had to stop singing. This doesn't happen very often, but I cherish the times when it does.

I sometimes wonder what it will be like to experience the latter rain. Frankly, I don't know. But that doesn't matter—trying to anticipate what it will be like can lead to false expectations. If you and I are pursuing revival and a relationship with Jesus now, we can be sure we'll receive the latter rain when it comes, and that will be soon enough for us to learn what it's like.

What I do know is that experiencing revival today is an essential preparation for receiving the latter rain then. We must have the assurance that God accepts us in spite of our faults. We must learn about Him and His plan for our lives through careful Bible study. We must develop a relationship with Him through daily prayer. And we must fellowship regularly with other believers. When we do these things, we *will* experience revival, and we *will* be ready for the latter rain when it comes.

As Mark Finley said, "The second coming of Christ may seem to be delayed, but our preparation for His return should never be delayed."

1. Mark Finley, *Revive Us Again* (Nampa, ID: Pacific Press®, 2010), 47.

2. White, *Last Day Events,* 183.

3. Marvin Moore, *Forever His* (Nampa, ID: Pacific Press®, 2004).

4. Marvin Moore, *Conquering the Dragon Within* (Nampa, ID: Pacific Press®, 2001), 13–92.

5. White, *Steps to Christ,* 62.

6. Ellen G. White, *Selected Messages* (Hagerstown, MD: Review and Herald®, 1958), 1:382.

7. *Bible Readings for the Home* (Mountain View, CA: Pacific Press®, 1963).

8. *Handbook of Seventh-day Adventist Theology* (Hagerstown, MD: Review and Herald®, 2000); also part of *The Seventh-day Adventist Bible Commentary* set.

9. *Seventh-day Adventists Believe* (Silver Spring, MD: General Conference Ministerial Association, 2005).

10. White, *Selected Messages,* 1:121.

11. Ellen G. White, *Gospel Workers* (Hagerstown, MD: Review and Herald®, 1958), 257.

12. White, *Testimonies for the Church,* 2:268.

CHAPTER 17

The Latter Rain: Reformation

Reformation means making the changes in our thinking and acting that will bring our lives up to the standard God has set, the standard revealed in the Bible. Reformation requires revival, but revival alone isn't enough. And if revival doesn't lead to reformation, it isn't genuine.

Justification and sanctification go hand in hand in the same way that revival and reformation do. Genuine justification leads to sanctification; and if justification doesn't produce sanctification, it isn't the real thing. In the previous chapter, we discussed the justification aspect of righteousness by faith. Now we need to discuss the sanctification aspect.

God doesn't demand that we be perfect before He will accept us, but He does ask for our loyalty to His commandments. Loyalty is extremely important to any close relationship because it helps us get through those times when we do something that displeases the person we love. Our loved one can accept our imperfection as long as he or she knows we are loyal to him or her and want to please him or her. That's the point behind the first part of a statement by Ellen White that I quoted in the previous chapter: "When it's in the heart to obey God, when efforts are put forth to this end . . ." Christians may not always be successful at obeying God, but they *want* to obey Him, and they *do their best* to obey Him. That's loyalty.

If we truly desire to serve God and we are doing our very best to serve Him, *we* will *make progress in our efforts to overcome*. That desire and effort and the progress they inevitably produce is what we call *sanctification*. In my book *Conquering the Dragon Within*, I give some practical suggestions about what people can do to aid their growth in sanctification. I'll summarize them in this chapter.

Praising God for victory is an important element in overcoming temptation. I consider praising Him for victory *at the right time* to be one of the most helpful things we can do to obtain victory. We typically think that we should praise God *after* we've met the temptation successfully, and of course that *is* a time for rejoicing. But I've found it extremely helpful to praise God for the victory when the temptation is burning in my heart, *before* the victory is mine. I've learned to say at that point, "God, I thank You for the victory that You've already given me over this sin. I thank You, Jesus, that You are with me, and because You are, this temptation has no power over me." Praying this at that time expresses faith that God *can* and *will* deliver us from the temptation we're facing.

Three more strategies for victory

I've found three other strategies critical to gaining the victory over temptation.

1. Ask God for insight. I do *not* understand all of my character defects. I'm blind to many of the things in my life that will need correction if I'm to remain faithful to God through the final crisis. Fortunately, He knows my spiritual needs, and He's anxious to help me understand them. That's why one of the most important things we can pray for is divine enlightenment about them. I can assure you that God will answer that prayer. We won't understand all our needs all at once, but as time goes on, we'll become aware of first one and then another of the imperfections in our lives that He wants us to overcome. Keep in mind that one of the most effective ways God has of revealing our character defects is to let them get us in trouble. So, when you've prayed for God to show your weaknesses to you, don't be surprised if life suddenly becomes a lot more painful. Instead of fretting about your problems or trying to run away from them, thank God for them, and ask Him to help you understand the lesson He wants you to learn.

All of us can also benefit from growth in our understanding of those character defects we *are* aware of. If you seem to be at a standstill in overcoming a particular problem, ask God to show you why, and then discuss the issue with a trusted friend. The very process of sharing the problem with another person will help you to understand it better. And whatever your struggle, I can assure you that others have experienced it before you, and you can benefit from their counsel.

Once you've asked God to show you the defects in your character, you can speed up the process by doing some spiritual research. The place to begin that research is, of course, the Bible. If you're struggling with a particular issue, look up everything you can find in the Bible about it, and reflect carefully on what you learn. Sometimes what you discover will surprise you—you'll be reading along and suddenly the words will jolt you: "Whoa! I'd never realized that about myself before!"

You can also learn a lot about yourself by reading current books about the character defect God has helped you to identify. Go to a bookstore, find the section on recovery, and then browse through the titles, looking for one or more books that deal with your temptation. Or type your issue into a search engine on the Web and see what you come up with. No doubt some of what you discover will tout New Age approaches to the problem. Ask God to help you screen out such material.

2. Deal with the desire. Why do we keep yielding to a particular temptation? *Because we want to!* We *love* doing what we're being tempted to do. If victory were simply a matter of making up our minds to quit, we'd all be victors every time. But we get this *urge* for whatever it is, and as long as we have that urge, we'll yield to it. Great determination and effort may enable us to resist that temptation for a while, and, as I'll point out in the next section of this chapter, there is a place for that kind of resistance. But making this our only approach to overcoming temptation raises two problems. First, as long as we continue to have the desire, we'll almost certainly yield to it occasionally regardless of how frequently and how loudly we say No! And second, even if we could successfully say No for the rest of our lives through sheer determination, we wouldn't have overcome a thing. Victory over sin isn't just a matter of refusing to do it. It also means *no longer wanting to do it.**

The realization that victory over sin means that we no longer desire what used to tempt us opens the way for us to understand and accept an extremely important fact: *we can't rid ourselves of our wrong desires.* Ellen White has pointed out that "our hearts are evil, and we cannot change them." Our efforts "may produce an outward correctness of behavior, but they cannot change the heart; they cannot purify the springs of life."[1]

So how can we be changed? "There must be a power working from within, a new life from above, before men can be changed from sin to holiness. That power is Christ."[2]

The key to victory is having God *change* your desires—*so ask Him to do so!* Sometimes God answers that prayer by removing the sinful desire immediately and permanently. You've likely heard of people who threw their cigarettes away and never wanted another one. But for every person like that there are a hundred who had to work at it for a year or for five years before they were successful.

A few pages back, I suggested that praising God for the victory before we've obtained it is a very helpful strategy for overcoming temptation. I suggest that you praise God for victory *while the temptation is burning in your soul.* You won't *feel* like God has removed the sinful desire, but praising Him for removing it is your act of faith that He *will* do so.

There are two circumstances in which it's especially helpful to ask God to remove a sinful desire. One is when we're *not* facing that temptation. We can just say, "God, please help me not to *want* _____" and name the temptation we're concerned about.

It's even more important that we pray the moment the temptation strikes us. It can be very difficult to do this because we *want* so badly to satisfy our desire *right now!* But it's then that we should exercise our will-power and pray for help to resist the temptation.

---

* I'm aware that some people who quit smoking say that years later they still want a cigarette. However, even for these people, the desire not to smoke is much stronger than an occasional sense of wanting a cigarette. I don't think that all day every day they're longing to smoke.

What should we do if the temptation is so strong that we can't bring ourselves to ask for help and so we give in to it?

In that case, we must confess our wrong and then ask God to give us the strength of will we need to ask Him to remove the desire the next time the temptation strikes. If we keep doing that, eventually we'll be able to say the prayer when we're under temptation.

We must also be alert to the first flickerings of the temptation. We may be tempted to play around with it, to enjoy it for a moment, with the idea that eventually we'll resist it. We mustn't do that! Instead, we should immediately ask God to remove the sinful desire. It's much easier for us to pray for help and for God to remove the desire when it's small than when it has set our soul ablaze.

Often, the wrong things we do cause us a lot of shame and guilt. Those emotions raise some of the greatest obstacles to overcoming sin. Ongoing shame and guilt will keep us bound to our sins; thus, one of the keys to spiritual victory is getting rid of these damaging emotions. That's why God begins His process of salvation with justification and forgiveness. He knows we can't overcome our temptations until we're free of our feelings of guilt about yielding to them time after time. You'll find it very helpful to discuss your besetting sins with someone who is nonjudgmental and whom you can trust to maintain confidences. You'll sense profound relief when this person listens to you and accepts you right where you are without condemning you. By doing so you can cut your shame in half. Jesus illustrated this principle with the woman caught in adultery. The first words He said to her were "neither do I condemn you." Thus He freed her from her guilt and shame, and only then did He say, "Go now and leave your life of sin" (John 8:11).

3. Deal with the behavior. To obtain victory over sin, we must *always* deal with the sinful desire first. But once we've asked God to rid us of that desire, we can immediately ask Him to give us the strength to avoid yielding to it. Paul said, "I can do all this through him who gives me strength" (Philippians 4:13). That's a behavior statement: "I can *do* all things." But Paul couldn't do everything he needed to do by himself. He needed Christ to give him the moral strength to change his behavior.

Here's an example of a prayer in which the petitioner asks for a change of behavior: "Jesus, You broke the power of this temptation on the cross. Thank You for giving me, right now, the power not to yield."

When we've asked God for insight and we've dealt with the desire, we've reached the place where it's appropriate for us to clench our fists and grit our teeth and say No! to the temptation. We need to beware of making this our *only* response to the temptation. As I pointed out earlier, it's just one part of the strategy that will lead us to victory; it's a short-term line of attack that we can use while the desire is fading. Once it's gone, the victory will basically be ours. However, if the temptation was to commit one of our besetting sins, we'll no doubt have to deal with it again. When that happens, we should again ask God to remove the desire, then clench our fists, say No, and refuse to yield.

Please note that there's no point in asking God to remove your desire for food and sex. He won't do it because He's the one who built those desires into you. He did it when He created you. However, He will help you deal with an *obsession* about food or sex.

God won't remove your ability to feel angry either. This surprises some Christians, because when they were children, someone told them that anger is sinful. However, again, God gave you the ability to feel anger when He created you. Rightly used, anger is a good emotion. It helps you to defend yourself when you are being abused, and it helps you to protect others when you see them being abused. Your anger becomes sinful only when you use it to abuse other people. This happens when you lose your temper and lash out with harsh words and/or physical violence.

You'll find it helpful to ask God to help you understand the difference between how He meant us to respond to the desires for food and sex and the feeling of anger that He gave us, on one hand, and, on the other hand, the distortions of these drives that cause us to misuse them. You'll need time to sort all this out, and you almost certainly won't make all the right decisions from the very first. God understands that, and He's willing to give you the time to grow in your ability to discriminate between the right and the wrong use of your feelings. *And He'll accept you in spite of the mistakes you make as you engage in this process.* Remember that "when it is in [your] heart to obey God, when [you put forth] efforts . . . to this end, Jesus accepts this desire and effort as [your] best effort, and He makes up for the deficiency with His own divine merit."[3]

This statement contains both justification and sanctification. While we tend to discuss them as separate processes, in real life they work together to help us develop a character patterned on Christ's. Someone once said that sanctification is simply a continual application of justification. This is indeed true! Justification means that through all of your ups and downs, your successes and failures, God is standing beside you, encouraging you, forgiving you, and guiding you into the right way of life. What counts with Him is the fact that you *want* to overcome, and you're doing your *best* to overcome. That last clause is the sanctification part.

I couldn't have said it better than Ellen White did in the following short statement: "Christ looks at the spirit, and when He sees us carrying our burden with faith, His perfect holiness atones for our shortcomings. *When we do our best, He becomes our righteousness.*"[4]

Conclusion

Revival and reformation are essential to our Christian experience. They're essential to our developing characters that will stand through the world's final crisis. If you ignore them now, you may not discover your need for them until it's too late. But if you're doing your best today, God will see to it that you're as ready as you need to be when the time comes. You won't have to worry about whether you're good enough to live without a Mediator after the close of probation.

---

1. White, *Steps to Christ*, 18.
2. Ibid.
3. White, *Selected Messages*, 1:382.
4. Ibid., p. 368; emphasis added.

CHAPTER 18

The Loud Cry

In Revelation 18:1, 2, John tells us he saw "another angel come down from heaven, having great power; and the earth was lightened with his glory. And he cried mightily with a strong voice, saying, Babylon the great is fallen, is fallen" (KJV). These two verses and the six that follow describe God's last call to the human race, just before the close of probation. Seventh-day Adventists sometimes refer to the proclamation of this message as the "loud cry." With the power and grace supplied in the latter rain and aided by all of our modern communication technology, God's people will proclaim the final warning message to the world.

Ellen White described this time. "During the loud cry," she said, "the church, aided by the providential interpositions of her exalted Lord, will diffuse the knowledge of salvation so abundantly that light will be communicated to every city and town. The earth will be filled with the knowledge of salvation. So abundantly will the renewing Spirit of God have crowned with success the intensely active agencies, that the light of present truth will be seen flashing everywhere."[1] While in this passage Ellen White pictured the loud cry as still in the future, she also spoke of it as a present reality. She said, for instance, "the third angel's message *is* swelling into a loud cry,"[2] and we need to be "getting the spirit of the loud cry"[3] now.

The previous two chapters of this book have dealt with the preparation that each of us needs to be making as individuals during the delay.

In view of the crisis that lies ahead, it's essential that we each be preparing for that time now, both spiritually and physically. If we haven't made adequate preparation, there's a significant chance that when the crisis strikes, we will yield to the pressures around us and abandon our faith.

However, personal preparation is not our only responsibility during the delay. It's essential that we also help others to prepare. In fact, to some degree we're becoming prepared ourselves when we help others to prepare. Jesus specifically instructed His people to serve others in two ways during the delay.

Sharing the good news

Just before Jesus ascended to heaven He told His twelve disciples, "You will be my witnesses . . . to the ends of the earth" (Acts 1:8). That's the first way in which He told us to serve others. And earlier, in what we call the Great Commission, He said, "Go and make disciples of all nations" (Matthew 28:19). That's the second way He wants us to serve others. Again, He told us to "go and make disciples," not "go and evangelize."

Notice that Jesus said, "You will be my *witnesses*," not "You will be my *evangelists*." I'm glad Jesus put it that way because I'm not an evangelist; so, I appreciate the fact that Jesus didn't say every Christian must preach and give Bible studies. But He does ask each person who looks to Him for salvation to be witnesses for Him, and He asks each of us to help others to become His disciples.

What does it mean to be a witness for Jesus? Witnessing is very simple— and it's fun! We're to make friends with people. One of the best places to begin is with our neighbors. Get to know the people who live near you. Stop and chat with them when you see them in their yards. And when it seems appropriate to do so, ask them if they grew up in a religious tradition. Listen to what they have to say about their religious background, and then share yours.

When a special occasion arises in your life, such as the birth of a child, a twenty-fifth anniversary, or a promotion on your job, invite them to celebrate with you. When you learn of a special occasion in their lives, celebrate with them. And organize a block party, inviting all of your neighbors to your home for an evening of food and fun.

As you become acquainted with your neighbors, you'll learn of the troubling issues some of them are dealing with. If someone is depressed or having marital problems, you can be a sympathetic listening ear. If someone is sick or dies, you can offer to help with meals and house cleaning, and if you have medical expertise, you may be able to help with simple home treatments.

And by all means you should also make friends of the people you work with, cultivating your relationship with them in much the same way you do with your neighbors.

Adventist churches receive lots of calls about nonmembers who are in need. Church members from other parts of the country call, asking for someone from your church to visit their son or daughter who's a patient in a local hospital. Make that visit! Or perhaps someone calls who's out of work and about out of food. This is an excellent opportunity to lend a sympathetic ear and to share some of the wealth God has blessed you with. And once you've established that friendship, keep it up. Pray for wisdom to say the right thing when spiritual and religious questions arise—which they almost certainly will. And when it's appropriate, invite these people to attend church with you.

Churches receive many calls from people who are traveling through town and have run out of money for gas or lodging. If you can afford it, go to a gas station with them and fill their tank, or take them to a low-cost motel and pay for a night's lodging. They would probably also appreciate a meal at a restaurant. You may never see these people again, but you will have shared a bit of kindness, and that will make a lasting impression on them about both you and the church you represent.

In most cases you won't know these people well enough to determine whether their need is genuine, but I've always followed the policy that I'd rather help someone who doesn't need help than fail to help someone who does. And who knows—some of these people may come up to you in heaven someday and thank you for getting them started on the pathway to salvation.

It's living this kind of helpful, caring life that Jesus was talking about when He said, "I was hungry and you gave me something to eat, I was thirsty and you gave me something to drink, I was a stranger and you invited me in, I needed clothes and you clothed me, I was sick and you looked after me, I was in prison and you came to visit me" (Matthew 25:35, 36). This is what it means to be a witness for Jesus.

We're not only to bear witness of Jesus, we're to "make disciples of all nations." That means we're to lead people to become active in serving Him. New believers especially need to be shown how to be active Christians. Again, this starts with being friends. Too many times we fall to the temptation of baptizing people and then forgetting about them. As long as they were prospective members, we visited regularly, gave them Bible studies, and invited them to attend church. But after they're baptized, our friendly initiatives end. Church growth experts tell us that to keep the newly baptized in the church, they must be connected to five or six individual church members and/or families. You are actually doing significant evangelism when you simply become good friends with the people who join your church and you keep in touch with them regularly.

Another way to integrate new members into the church is to give them something to do for the church. As you become acquainted with them, you'll learn what their talents are. Perhaps they play an instrument. If so, invite them to give special music for Sabbath School or church. Are they party people? Involve them in planning your church's social activities. Do they maintain a neat yard? Let them help keep up the church's grounds. If you give Bible studies, take them with you. As new members become integrated into the church, ask them to make hospital visits and to call on people who ask the church for help. In time, these new members will become old members who take on greater responsibilities as deaconesses, elders, Sabbath School teachers, and so forth.

Most of us have very busy lifestyles, so you won't be able to do all of the things I've suggested, but you can do some of them. Becoming involved with people is what Jesus meant when He called us to be His witnesses and to make disciples. Using some of our time and occasionally some of our money to become friends with people is part of what it means to be Christians. It's also very enjoyable and satisfying.

Evangelism

Some people tense up when they hear the word *evangelism*. They think it means preaching doctrinal sermons and giving doctrinal Bible studies, and they say, "We can't do that." Preaching and giving Bible studies certainly comprises a part of what we call evangelism. However, in the letters Paul wrote to three of the New Testament churches, he mentioned at least nineteen spiritual gifts: being apostles, prophets, evangelists, pastors, or teachers; having wisdom, knowledge, or faith; being able to heal, perform miracles, prophesy, discern spirits, speak in more than one language, interpret a foreign language, serve others, encourage others, give generously, provide leadership, or show mercy (see Ephesians 4:11; 1 Corinthians 12:8–10; Romans 12:6–8). Now please notice that only one of these gifts is evangelism. Some people love to conduct public meetings and to give Bible studies. That's because God gave them the gift of evangelism, and they should use that gift to serve Him. People who preach publicly and give Bible studies to unbelievers are witnessing for Jesus and making disciples for Him. *But God doesn't ask people to be evangelists if He hasn't given them the gift of evangelism.*

This doesn't mean, however, that you can sit back and let the people with the gift of evangelism do all the work. Holding public evangelistic meetings successfully requires the various skills of many people. Are you trained in some field of medical work? Many evangelists like to have a health talk during the meetings. Are you comfortable speaking in public? Evangelists need people to make announcements, offer prayer, and give special music. Are you good at electronics? You can help with the public address system or with the evangelist's PowerPoint program. Are you good at keeping records? There's a vital need for that skill in keeping track of the names and addresses of the people who attend meetings. Are you warm and outgoing? Do you enjoy meeting new people? You can be part of a team that calls on the visitors who attend the meetings, or you can be a greeter who welcomes visitors as they enter the church. Evangelists need people to distribute handouts to the audience during the meetings. Most evangelists sell books before and after their nightly meetings, so they need one or two people to make the transactions and to handle the money. And there's a need for someone to come early to open the doors and to stay late to close them when everyone else has left. These people also have to check the heating or cooling system, distribute copies of the evening sermon, and be sure the restrooms are clean and well stocked. *You are participating in evangelism when you help with these things.*

Another excellent way to do evangelism is to send subscriptions to Adventist missionary magazines to your friends, neighbors, and coworkers. *Message, El Centinela*®, and *Signs of the Times*® are the full-message missionary journals that have been developed for people in North America, and all of them have a significant readership in other parts of the world too. *El Centinela*® is prepared for Hispanic readers, *Message* for African American readers, and *Signs of the Times*® for anyone who can read English. These magazines cover all of the teachings of the Seventh-day Adventist Church on a regular basis.*

One advantage that subscribing to these missionary journals for people you're concerned about is that they can go where you can't, and they can go there year after year after year. You may have friends or relatives who live so far away that you can't visit them frequently. It's also probable that most of the friends and relatives who live near you would feel that you were being intrusive if you were to visit them regularly to talk about religion. But, month by month, the missionary magazines offer a quiet, inoffensive witness, nurturing people in their Christian walk and helping them to learn more about the Seventh-day Adventist faith.†

Because these magazines provide a regular, effective witness, I also recommend that you suggest to your church board that your church sponsor subscriptions to them for everyone who has shown interest in the Seventh-day Adventist Church—people who have taken Bible studies or who have attended your evangelistic meetings. Someone from the church can phone or visit these people annually and ask how they're

---

* As editor of *Signs of the Times*®, I make it a point to cover all of the major teachings of the Seventh-day Adventist Church at least once a year and most of them several times a year. We have at least one article dealing with some aspect of salvation and the spiritual life in every issue.

† *Signs of the Times*® and *El Centinela*® are published monthly. *Message* is published every other month.

enjoying the magazines they're receiving. If they say they love it and read every issue cover to cover, or even if they say they read it when they have the time, keep the subscription going. If they say they seldom or never read it, transfer the subscription to someone else.

Suppose you do feel God's call to give Bible studies or to preach evangelistic meetings. Ask your pastor or someone else who's giving Bible studies to take you with them. After you've observed a few, try giving one yourself with your mentor present. In due time you'll be able to start giving Bible studies on your own, and when you've developed some skill at it, you can, in turn, train someone else.

If you feel called to preach, try starting out with a Revelation Seminar or a small group in a Sabbath School classroom. Call ShareHim* and ask for their material. The staff of ShareHim also conducts training seminars at various locations throughout the United States.

Foreign missions

For the first 125 years of our church's existence, it took so long to travel to and from distant parts of the world that people were not accepted as foreign missionaries unless they agreed to spend several years working at the mission station to which they were assigned. The church still needs people who want to spend their lives in foreign mission service. If you feel called to dedicate your life or even just a few years of your life to this kind of mission service, by all means get in touch with the General Conference of Seventh-day Adventists and let them know of your interest.†

However, these days, with the right itinerary, people can get to most any place on earth within twenty-four to forty-eight hours. This has made other forms of foreign mission service practical and affordable. So, today, thousands of Adventists are volunteering for short-term foreign mission trips that last anywhere from two weeks to three or four months.

In the past few years, my wife and I have conducted numerous public

---

* ShareHim is a ministry that trains people to do evangelism. It was developed by former General Conference president Robert Folkenberg, who specializes in preparing PowerPoint programs that make it easy to preach evangelistic sermons. You can reach him by calling 1-877-8-SHARE-8.

† The General Conference telephone number is 301-680-6000.

evangelistic meetings in India. We fly out of Boise, Idaho, conduct a two-week-long series of meetings that pulls in people from several villages, and three weeks after we left home, we're back. We use the Power-Point programs provided by ShareHim. These programs display on the speaker's laptop monitor the same image that the audience is seeing on the screen—with one significant difference: the text that appears on the computer monitor is in English; what appears on the audience's screen is in the local language! Each of the meetings we've held has resulted in the baptism of several hundred people.

Another excellent way to do foreign mission service is to help build Adventist schools and churches in underdeveloped countries of the world. Maranatha Volunteers International is a lay Adventist organization that builds hundreds of schools and churches around the world every year.* Often, the people working on these building projects conduct public evangelistic meetings in the evening as well. Volunteers can help with either aspect of these events.

Money

When Bob Kyte was president of Pacific Press (1989–2005), he used to tell the employees, "Our mission is not money, but without money there is no mission." Some people complain that churches are constantly asking for money. They're right! But it takes money to heat and cool the building, maintain the church yard, keep the inside of the church clean, and provide Sabbath School quarterlies for the adults and magazines for the children's departments.† It takes money to pay the salaries of ministers and other leaders at the various levels of church organization. It takes money to operate elementary schools, academies, colleges, and universities. It takes money to conduct evangelistic meetings, Revelation Seminars, and health classes for the public. And it takes money to send missionaries to foreign countries, whether they are long term or short term. All of these services depend on the generous offerings of church members.

---

* For information about serving with Maranatha Volunteers International, go to www.maranatha.org and click on the Contact link.

† *Our Little Friend®, Primary Treasure®, Guide,* and *Insight.*

Then there are the times when we meet someone in need. We can buy a meal, purchase a tank of gas, pay a utility bill, or help someone with their rent. Needs are everywhere, and no one can do it all, but each of us can do something.

Time and money are two of the most valuable assets each of us has. Some people can give more of one; some can give more of the other. God asks us to give *some* of our time and *some* of our means to Him.

In this chapter and the two previous ones, we've discussed revival, reformation, and the loud cry—our personal relationship with Christ and our responsibility to share Him with others. While it's helpful to understand these events individually, it's also crucial to bring them together, for only those who have a close personal relationship with Jesus can share Him with others.

The latter rain and the loud cry are not simply theological and eschatological concepts. They are deeply spiritual realities that God wants every one of His people to experience. Indeed, we cannot be a part of the loud cry *unless* we are experiencing the revival and reformation of the latter rain. Once we have experienced the latter rain, the loud cry will follow as surely as spring and summer follow winter. However, we shouldn't wait for some powerful spiritual experience before we begin to witness and make disciples for Jesus. Revival, reformation, and proclamation must go hand in hand.

Are you anxious to see the end of the delay? Do you long for Jesus to take you to our heavenly home? Then *make* the time to read your Bible and to pray. And when you've been nourished spiritually, get off your knees and get involved in the ministry of your local church and maybe even the worldwide church, using the spiritual gifts and financial resources that God has blessed you with.

Together, we *can* hasten the end of the delay!

---

1. Ellen G. White, *Review and Herald,* October 13, 1904, 7, cited in *Evangelism* (Hagerstown, MD: Review and Herald®, 1946), 694.

2. Ellen G. White, *God's Amazing Grace* (Hagerstown, MD: Review and Herald®, 1973), 205; emphasis added.

3. White, *Evangelism,* 405.

CHAPTER 19

Healthful Living

On my mother's side, I'm a fifth-generation Seventh-day Adventist. My grandmother, Anna Gilbert, used to enjoy telling a story about her grandparents—my great-great-grandparents—who were first-generation Adventists. My great-great-grandparents lived in Battle Creek, Michigan, and their next-door neighbors were James and Ellen White. It seems that one day the Whites decided to drop in on their neighbors for a visit, and apparently, they didn't want to go empty-handed, so, as a token of their friendship, they brought a side of ham! (Or it may have been the other way around—perhaps the neighbors brought the ham to the Whites.)

I know that sounds hard to believe, given the Seventh-day Adventist conviction that pork is unclean meat. However, if this story is true, it probably tells us something about when my great-great-grandparents were neighbors of the Whites. It had to have been before June 1863, for it was on the sixth day of that month that the Whites were visiting in the home of a Brother Hilliard in Otsego, Michigan, and Mrs. White received her comprehensive health vision.[1]

Healthful living was not given much attention in the early days of the Adventist movement. Nevertheless, there was some interest in the topic. James and Ellen White took a public stand against tobacco, tea, and coffee as early as 1848. In 1851, Mrs. White stated that her angel had showed her that tobacco was an idol and it was " 'high time it was given up.' "[2] By 1853, the *Review and Herald* was publishing frequent articles against tobacco, and in 1855, the Vermont Conference voted to disfellowship those who used that toxic weed[3]—though a year later, because of strong opposition, they replaced that resolution with one that encouraged Adventists "perseveringly to persuade each brother and sister who indulge in the use of it, to abstain."[4]

During the 1850s, a number of church members were advocating that Adventists drop swine's flesh from their diet—some of them making such a crusade of it that they created considerable dissension. In response, on October 21, 1858, Ellen White counseled these advocates, "I saw that your views concerning swine's flesh would prove no injury if you have them to yourselves; but in your judgment and opinion you have made this question a test, and your actions have plainly shown your faith in this matter. If God requires His people to abstain from swine's flesh, He will convict them on the matter."[5]

Joseph Bates had given up alcohol and tobacco even before he accepted the Sabbath,[6] and he was among the first Adventists to adopt a vegetarian diet and discontinue the use of highly spiced and greasy foods.[7] However, he was considered something of an oddity in church circles, and when he realized that his convictions were not shared, he resorted to witnessing by the example he set.[8] For the most part, these early Adventists concerned themselves with preaching the soon coming of Jesus, the Sabbath, the state of the dead, and other doctrines that they considered more crucial than healthful living.

Then came Ellen White's vision on health reform, and none too soon. Poor health habits were taking their toll on Seventh-day Adventists, including their leaders. James White suffered a stroke in August 1865, and John Loughborough was unable to walk without experiencing severe head pains.[9] Indeed, for nearly a year, the governing committees of both the General Conference and the Michigan Conference couldn't conduct official business because so many of their committee members were sick that they couldn't meet the required quorums![10]

During the latter part of 1865, in an effort to recover their health, the Whites, John Loughborough, and Uriah Smith spent three months at the Dansville Home, a health reform institution operated by a Dr. James C. Jackson. Then, on December 25, 1865, Ellen White received another vision on health reform in which she was instructed, among other things, that Seventh-day Adventists should establish their own health reform institution "for the afflicted and those who wish to learn how to take care of their bodies that they may prevent sickness."[11] The result was the Western Health Reform Institute, which was launched with $2,625 of seed money.[12] Under the leadership of the brilliant John Harvey Kellogg, the institution, later renamed the Battle Creek Sanitarium, grew until it was the largest of its kind in the world.[13] The patient count grew from 106 in 1866 to 7,006 in 1906. Among its many patients were such famous people as Mary Todd Lincoln and J. C. Penney.[14]

Today, the Seventh-day Adventist Church operates 167 hospitals and sanitariums around the world, including the Loma Linda Medical Center. Loma Linda University, on the same campus as the medical center, is the denomination's premier health institution, providing schools of medicine, dentistry, nursing, and training in a variety of other health-related fields.

What does all of this have to do with the delay? I'll mention two things.

The mind-body connection

My first pastorate after I graduated from seminary and completed my internship was in the wind-blown town of Mojave, California. During my four years there, I became fairly well acquainted with the local Nazarene preacher. One day when I was visiting him in his home, our conversation turned to the topic of healthful living, and my friend made a statement I've never forgotten. He said, "All I care about is the soul. The condition of the body doesn't matter to me."

A Seventh-day Adventist would never say that, because we don't believe that the soul exists as a conscious entity apart from the body. As we understand it, our mental and emotional faculties have their source in our brains, as do our moral understanding and our spiritual nature. When the brain ceases to function, the mental, emotional, moral, and spiritual aspects of our nature also cease to function. In order to have the clearest minds and the most well-balanced emotions, we must have healthy bodies and healthy brains. When the body suffers, so does the brain—and with it, our ability to reason well, to exercise our will properly, and to commune with God and conform our lives to His moral principles.

Paul wrote that our bodies are temples for the Holy Spirit to dwell in (1 Corinthians 3:16, 17). If our brains are functioning at less than ideal capacity, our relationship with God will be affected. And anything that damages our health hinders clear thinking. In other words, our relationship with God will be less than ideal if we compromise our physical health.

Chapters 16 and 17 of this book dealt with revival and reformation—two spiritual experiences that we *must* be cultivating right now in order to be prepared for the final crisis when it comes. While we may die before the final crisis and thus escape it, we can't be sure of that. Therefore, it's essential that we prepare for that crisis now, during the delay. But if our bodies are unhealthy, then our brains will also be unhealthy, our moral and spiritual powers will be weak, and our abilities to engage in revival and reformation will be compromised. Thus, keeping our bodies healthy is essential to revival and reformation. To a man who considered the Adventist teaching about healthful living to be a "needless appendix to the truth," Ellen White said, "It is not so; it is a part of the truth."[15] And later, she wrote, "It is just as much sin to violate the laws of our being as to break one of the Ten Commandments."[16] *This is the primary reason why the Adventist health message is crucial to our spiritual well-being right now.*

Here's a list of the primary elements of the Adventist health message:

- A diet that emphasizes fruits, vegetables, grains, and nuts. While not a condition of membership, a vegetarian diet is highly recommended.
- Vigorous daily exercise
- Fresh air

- Adequate rest
- Plenty of water
- Abstinence from alcohol, tobacco, tea, coffee, and nonprescription narcotics*
- An optimistic outlook on life

Sharing the gospel of health

Seventh-day Adventists believe that God called us to be the John the Baptists of our day. Just as the primary responsibility of this biblical forerunner was to prepare the way for Christ's first coming (Matthew 3:1–3), so ours is to prepare the way for His second coming. We are to proclaim all of the basic truths of Christianity, especially salvation by faith alone through Christ. In addition, God has given us a special understanding of several neglected Bible truths: the Sabbath, the nature of man (particularly, our state in death), the great controversy, the sanctuary, the investigative judgment, and certain key biblical prophecies—especially Christ's second coming.

However, we are not simply to bring people to an intellectual acknowledgment of these doctrines. We are to lead them into a close personal relationship with Jesus that will give them peace of mind (Romans 5:1), a revived spirituality, and reformation of character. And in order to lead people into an intimate relationship with Jesus, we must teach them the laws of health and encourage them to live by them. That's why health evangelism is second only to gospel evangelism.

Seventh-day Adventists sometimes refer to health evangelism as "the right arm of the message." Ellen White wrote,

> Medical missionary work and the gospel are one. If united, they make a complete whole.[17]

> Again and again, I have been instructed that the medical missionary work is to bear the same relation to the work of the third angel's message that the arm and hand bear to the body. Under

---

* Prescription narcotics are also easily abused and should be used judiciously.

the direction of the divine Head they are to work unitedly in preparing the way for the coming of Christ. The right arm of the body of truth is to be constantly active, constantly at work, and God will strengthen it. But it is not to be made the body. At the same time the body is not to say to the arm, "I have no need of thee." The body has need of the arm in order to do active, aggressive work. Both have their appointed work, and each will suffer great loss if worked independently of the other.[18]

In addition to its spiritual importance, health evangelism has a very practical significance: many people will attend a presentation on health who wouldn't dream of coming to one of our church services or evangelistic meetings. While Western nations have very advanced health care systems, in many cases the overall health of their citizens falls behind that of people who live in some of the least-developed parts of the world. Obesity, heart disease, and cancer are rampant. That being the case, many people in developed countries are concerned about their health and want to learn how to improve it. Adventist health ministry can make a contribution not only to our own church but to the well-being of the communities in which we live—and by doing so, it can break down people's prejudices and open their minds and hearts to the reception of other truths that we teach.

So if you are trained in some aspect of health, I urge you to become involved in your church's health evangelism. And if your church doesn't have a health evangelism program now, take the lead in getting one started. There are all kinds of possibilities:

- Cooking schools
- Weight-loss classes
- Stop-smoking classes
- Stress-management classes
- Classes on dealing with depression and anxiety
- Christian 12-step meetings
- Health screenings (blood pressure, weight, bone density, blood sugar, etc.)

The Coronary Health Improvement Project (CHIP) is a very popular Adventist health education program that was developed by Dr. Hans Diehl. Classes are held four times a week for thirty days, and they cover total lifestyle, including but not limited to proper nutrition. Before the classes begin, participants are given a health screening that includes their weight, blood pressure, and total blood count (including cholesterol and blood sugar). Then, at the close of the program, the participants are given another health screening, which shows them how their health has improved as a result of their participation in the program.*

You don't have to be medically trained in order to conduct a CHIP program, so, to ensure that the CHIP programs held in local churches meet the standards of excellence, CHIP provides leadership training that prepares the teams of the local churches to conduct the classes. This training covers everything a church needs to do in order to conduct a successful program. Those who don't wish to lead out can participate by helping with registration, serving as table hosts, and assisting in the kitchen with the cooking classes.

Another form of health evangelism

If you and your church really wish to get ambitious, try conducting a health fair. The church I attend, in Caldwell, Idaho, did that in the fall of 2010. We called it "Health Expo." We contacted about forty health-related agencies and businesses in the area and invited them to participate. A local mall provided space for the event at no charge.† Several of the agencies and businesses conducted classes on topics such as weight loss, depression, diabetes, and exercises for osteoporosis. Church members checked blood pressure, height and weight, and lung capacity, and the personnel of a drugstore provided blood glucose testing. One of the popular features of this Health Expo was the cooking class held each evening in the mall corridor. We provided samples of the dishes that

---

* For information about CHIP, including a list of leadership classes and class locations, go to www.SDAchip.com.

† The health fair benefitted the mall by attracting people who then spent money at the various shops.

were demonstrated so people could taste them.

Many health-related agencies and businesses set up booths in the mall corridor, including a chiropractor, an organic food outlet, the dairy association, the local YMCA, the county health department, the National Association for Mental Illness, and on and on. The fair ran for three full days, from 10 A.M. to 9 P.M. Church members helped by setting up chairs and tables, registering visitors as they came in, assisting with the classes conducted by the church, and walking the halls just to be sure everyone and everything was cared for.

Putting on a health fair requires about the same amount of time and effort as does a public evangelistic series. But health fairs cost a lot less to run. A full-blown evangelistic series conducted by a professional evangelist can cost as much as a hundred thousand dollars, but often a church can produce a health fair for five thousand dollars or less, especially if the mall provides the space free of charge.

Are you anxious to see Jesus come? Would you like to see the end of the delay? Then urge your church to become involved in health evangelism. When you support your church's health-related outreach activities, you are just as certainly participating in evangelism as if you were giving Bible studies or preaching evangelistic sermons.

1. Spalding, *Origin and History of Seventh-day Adventists,* 1:345.

2. Ellen G. White, Letter 5, 1851, to Brother Barnes, December 14, 1851, cited in *Manuscript Releases* (Silver Spring, MD: Ellen G. White Estate, 1993), 5:377.

3. Spalding, *Origin and History of Seventh-day Adventists,* 1:338.

4. *Review and Herald,* December 4, 1855; *Review and Herald,* March 5, 1857; cited by Spalding, *Origin and History of Seventh-day Adventists,* 1:338.

5. White, *Testimonies for the Church,* 1:206, 207.

6. George Knight, *Joseph Bates: The Real Founder of Seventh-day Adventism* (Hagerstown, MD: Review and Herald®, 2004), 44.

7. Spalding, *Origin and History of Seventh-day Adventists,* 1:336.

8. Ibid.

9. Ibid., 1:354.

10. Ibid., 1:355.

11. White, *Testimonies for the Church,* 1:489; see also Spalding, *Origin and History of Seventh-day Adventists,* 1:365.

12. Spalding, *Origin and History of Seventh-day Adventists,* 1:368, 369.

13. Ibid., 2:223.

14. http://en.wikipedia.org/wiki/Battle_Creek_Sanitarium#Guests.2C_staff.2C_and _buildings.

15. White, *Testimonies for the Church,* 1:546.

16. Ibid., 2:70.

17. Ellen G. White, Letter 92, 1902, cited in *Manuscript Releases,* 1:228.

18. White, *Testimonies for the Church,* 6:288.

PART 5

The End of the Delay

CHAPTER 20

Nearing the End of the Delay

I'm sure you've heard people say that they believe Jesus will return within the next five years. I mentioned in a previous chapter that I first heard that opinion expressed back in about 1956. My response then, and ever since, has always been to point to the prophecies about the final years of earth's history as given in Scripture and in the writings of Ellen White. The most significant is the prediction in Revelation 13 that the United States will lead the world in establishing a theocracy that will persecute religious dissenters with an iron fist. It seems to me that the political process required for that to develop is too complex for it to happen in the next five years.

I'm aware, of course, that the natural disasters that Scripture and Ellen White inform us will occur during the final crisis* could push that process into high gear. However, until we see those calamities actually happening, we must base our opinions about "how near is near" on what we *do* see, and in my opinion, what we see makes it highly unlikely that the prophesied global religious intolerance could develop within the next five years.

This doesn't mean that we are left with no indication that Christ's second coming is near. However, I believe that present trends have greater significance as general portents than as fulfillments of specific prophecies.

* I discuss these natural disasters in detail in my book *The Coming Great Calamity.*

Each event is a part of a trend, and it's the trend that we need to pay attention to. In chapters 7 through 11 of this book, I pointed out five trends that have developed within the past several decades that make me confident that Christ's return is indeed near:

1. The fact that we now have the technology for global communication and travel that makes it possible to finish very rapidly the task of proclaiming the gospel to the whole world (see Matthew 24:14).

2. The growing influence of spiritualism in our culture in fulfillment of biblical and Spirit of Prophecy predictions about deceptive demonic forces that will be unleashed in the world just before the end of time (see 2 Thessalonians 2:9, 10; Revelation 13:13, 14; 16:12–14; *The Great Controversy*, 624).

3. The growing political power of the papacy in fulfillment of Revelation 13:7, which states that the beast power will be given political authority "over every tribe, people, language and nation."

4. The growing political power of Religious Right Protestants in the United States, and the bitter attacks on church-state separation that they have been making since about 1980 that threaten to bring to an end the historic American principle of religious freedom and to open the way for religious intolerance (see Revelation 13:11–18; *The Great Controversy*, 582–592; *Testimonies for the Church*, 5:451).

5. The willingness of Christians in America to hold such profound prejudices against Muslims that Christians persecute them by burning their holy book, the Koran, and campaign to prevent them from building houses of worship.

I encourage Seventh-day Adventists to watch these trends. However, I believe that certain developments that are still in the future will constitute further evidence of the nearness of the end. I will mention five.

Development 1: Sunday laws

The passage and enforcement of Sunday laws will be one of the most dramatic of these developments. Ellen White wrote,

> By the decree enforcing the institution of the papacy in violation of the law of God [a Sunday law], our nation will disconnect herself fully from righteousness. When Protestantism shall stretch her hand across the gulf to grasp the hand of the Roman power; when she shall reach over the abyss to clasp hands with spiritualism; when, under the influence of this threefold union, our country shall repudiate every principle of its Constitution as a Protestant and republican government, and shall make provision for the propagation of papal falsehoods and delusions, then we may know that the time has come for the marvelous working of Satan and that the end is near.[1]

In this statement Ellen White clearly was speaking of a *national* Sunday law and not state and local Sunday laws, which local governmental bodies produce from time to time. She said, "Our *country* [will] repudiate every principle of its *Constitution.*" My conclusion is that when the United States Congress enacts a national Sunday law, "then we may know . . . that the end is near"; then we'll have more concrete evidence that it's near than we do today.

Yet even then, predictions about "the next five years" will probably be unwise. A careful examination of Ellen White's comments suggests that at first, this Sunday legislation will be rather mild, but that it will become increasingly harsh as time goes on. She spoke, for example, of Sunday laws as a *movement,* not a single event.[2] She also advised that when Sunday laws are first enacted, we should refrain from ordinary work on that day, devoting it instead to missionary work.[3] As time goes on, discrimination against Sabbath keepers will increase to the point that "some of them will be thrust into prison, some will be exiled, some will be treated as slaves."[4] Eventually, as the decree issued by the various rulers of Christendom against commandment keepers shall withdraw the protection of government and abandon them to those who desire their destruction, the people of God will flee from the cities and villages and associate together in companies, dwelling in the most desolate and solitary places. Many will find refuge in the strongholds of the mountains.[5]

Clearly, even when Sunday legislation becomes a reality, it will be as a developing political process rather than a single event.

Having said this, I will also note that I believe the enactment of a Sunday law by the United States Congress will be a very significant event, one that will definitely signal that the delay is nearing its end. Ellen White herself said in the statement I quoted above that when the United States enacts a Sunday law, we can "know . . . that the end is near."

Development 2: The judgments of God

Imagine how overwhelming it would have been if 2004's tsunami in the Indian Ocean, 2005's Hurricane Katrina, and the 2010–2011 earthquakes in Haiti, Chile, and Japan had all occurred within a single year—along with fifteen or twenty other calamities of equal or greater magnitude. The world would have been overwhelmed! This, I believe, is what will happen when God unleashes the four winds (see Revelation 7:1–4). It's what Jesus meant when He said that as a result of signs in the sun, moon, and stars, the nations would be "in anguish and perplexity," and people's hearts would fail them for fear (Luke 21:25, 26).* It's what Ellen White was referring to when she said, "Calamities will come—calamities most awful, most unexpected; and these destructions will follow one after another."[6]

Mrs. White pointed out that these natural disasters will in fact push into high gear the movement to make Sunday sacred:

---

* For a more detailed account of these natural disasters, see my book *The Coming Great Calamity,* 14–60.

The great deceiver will persuade men that those who serve God are causing these evils [natural disasters]. The class that have provoked the displeasure of Heaven will charge all their troubles upon those whose obedience to God's commandments is a perpetual reproof to transgressors. It will be declared that men are offending God by the violation of the Sunday sabbath; that this sin has brought calamities which will not cease until Sunday observance shall be strictly enforced; and that those who present the claims of the fourth commandment, thus destroying reverence for Sunday, are troublers of the people, preventing their restoration to divine favor and temporal prosperity.[7]

I believe that the onslaught of these natural disasters together with the Sunday legislation they prompt will constitute a second clear indication that the end truly is near. Yet even then I would caution against guessing God's timetable or concluding that Jesus will come "within the next five years." Please understand: I'm not saying that Christ *won't* come within five years of the passage of Sunday laws and the pouring out of the judgments of God. I'm just saying we won't *know* that He's coming within five years. The final crisis prior to the close of probation may very well last longer than that. As the difficulties and trials of God's people increase during this time, these "five-year" predictions could easily discourage those whose faith isn't yet mature.

Development 3: The latter rain and the loud cry

Some people say that the world's population is growing faster than our evangelistic efforts, and that if something doesn't change, we'll never get the gospel to every human being. I challenge that statement. Please note the following statistics:

- In 1870, there was one Seventh-day Adventist for every 250,000 people in the world.
- In 1930, there was one Seventh-day Adventist for every 6,500 people in the world.

- In 1990, there was one Seventh-day Adventist for every 795 people in the world.
- In 2010, there was one Seventh-day Adventist for every 407 people in the world.

These numbers tell me that our message *is* reaching the world. I'm sure we could have done the job much more rapidly, but with God's blessing, we *are* making progress. And we aren't the only ones proclaiming the gospel. Thousands of Baptists, Methodists, Pentecostals, and others are doing so too. While Seventh-day Adventists disagree with these people regarding certain doctrines, we have always recognized that there are genuine Christians in other denominations and that their witness for Jesus is also genuine.

Having said this, we must also recognize that a time is coming when the Holy Spirit will be poured out in latter-rain abundance and the gospel will be preached throughout the world with a power that we haven't yet seen in our day. This will be the "loud cry" of the angel of Revelation 18:1 that will illuminate the entire earth with God's splendor.

In the 1960s, 1970s, and early 1980s, people were asking how God was ever going to reach the atheistic Communist world with the gospel. Then came the dramatic events of the last half of 1989, when Eastern Europe broke free of Communism. The Berlin Wall collapsed in November of that year, and by the end of 1991, the Soviet Union no longer existed. Shortly after that, Mark Finley preached an evangelistic series *in the Kremlin* to thousands of Russians who hungered for spiritual nourishment.

Today, I hear the same question being asked about the countries of the Middle East and North Africa, Pakistan, and Indonesia: how is God going to break open the Muslim world? I don't know. However, I *am* certain that He has a plan. And from reports that I receive from time to time in my office at Pacific Press, I know that thousands of Muslims are accepting Jesus every year, often because of visions and dreams they have had. In some of these countries, Christians are severely persecuted, yet the conversions keep coming.

I also know that under the powerful influence of the latter rain and the loud cry, God is going to inspire His people to finish the proclamation of the gospel in a blaze of glory. While we mustn't put off proclaiming the gospel around the world until that happens, I can assure you that when it does, we will know it. And that, to me, will be another sign that the end truly is near.*

Development 4: The close of probation

Nobody will know when the investigative judgment now going on in the heavenly courts will end and probation closes. We won't hear Jesus proclaim the solemn words, "He who is unjust, let him be unjust still; he who is filthy, let him be filthy still; he who is righteous, let him be righteous still; he who is holy, let him be holy still" (Revelation 22:11, NKJV). Ellen White said, "God has not revealed to us the time when this message will close or when probation will have an end."[8]

Nevertheless, I believe that shortly *after* probation has closed, God's people will become aware that it has happened. My reason for this conclusion is that the close of probation will be the signal for seven of heaven's angels to begin pouring out the seven last plagues upon the earth. Revelation 15 describes the close of probation,† and John's portrayal of the seven last plagues follows immediately, in chapter 16.

The first plague will cause a skin disease to afflict all those who have received the mark of the beast (Revelation 16:2). If this plague is to be understood literally—and I believe I'm safe in saying that Seventh-day Adventists generally have understood it to be taken literally—then it seems to me that we will recognize it when it happens. This will be an indication that the end truly is near.

---

* Yet I should caution you that even then, some people will miss it! Ellen White said, "Unless we are daily advancing in the exemplification of the active Christian virtues, we shall not recognize the manifestations of the Holy Spirit in the latter rain. It may be falling on hearts all around us, but we shall not discern or receive it" (*Last Day Events,* 195, 196).

† For a detailed explanation of Revelation 15 and its relationship to the close of probation, see my book *How to Think About the End Time,* 144, 145.

Development 5: The death decree

A further development indicative that Jesus' return is just ahead will be the issuance of a global decree sentencing Sabbath keepers to death. In the chapter titled "The Time of Trouble" in *Early Writings,* Ellen White said,

> I saw a writing, copies of which were scattered in different parts of the land, giving orders that unless the saints should yield their peculiar faith, give up the Sabbath, and observe the first day of the week, the people were at liberty after a certain time to put them to death.[9]

Apparently, this death decree will be proclaimed shortly before the third plague is poured out, or perhaps just before the second. I say this because following the outpouring of the third plague an angel will proclaim, "You are just in these judgments, O Holy One, you who are and who were; for they have shed the blood of your holy people and your prophets, and you have given them blood to drink as they deserve" (Revelation 16:5, 6). Commenting on these verses, Ellen White said, "By condemning the people of God to death, they have as truly incurred the guilt of their blood as if it had been shed by their hands."[10]

Jesus' statement that no one knows the day or the hour of His coming applies right up to His return. However, I believe that when the death decree is issued, we can know that He will return *prior to* a particular date; we just won't know exactly how long before that date. I say this because of Ellen White's statement quoted in the paragraph above that "the people were at liberty *after a certain time* to put them [believers] to death." However, she also made it clear that Christ's second coming will deliver His people from this threat.[11] Thus, when this death decree is issued, which will include either a specific date or a specific length of time following the issuing of the decree,* we can be sure that Christ's second

---

* Ellen White's statement suggests the latter. She said that people will be at liberty "after a certain time" to put the saints to death. Once we know the length of that "certain time," we'll be able to calculate when that death decree goes into effect, and we'll know then that Christ will return no later than that date.

coming will occur before the slaughter it authorizes is carried out.

At that time we will know that the delay in Christ's return truly is almost over.

1. White, *Testimonies for the Church,* 5:451.

2. White, *The Great Controversy,* 448, 580, 607.

3. White, *Testimonies for the Church,* 9:232.

4. White, *The Great Controversy,* 608.

5. Ibid., 626.

6. Ellen G. White, Manuscript 35, 1906, cited in *Evangelism,* 27.

7. White, *The Great Controversy,* 590.

8. White, *Selected Messages,* 1:191.

9. White, *Early Writings,* 282, 283.

10. White, *The Great Controversy,* 628.

11. See chapter 40, "God's People Delivered," especially page 635, of White, *The Great Controversy.*

ADDENDUM:

How Long Will the Time of Trouble Last?

Adventists have traditionally said that the time of trouble will last about one year. This conclusion is based on the statement in Revelation 18:8 that the plagues on Babylon will occur "in one day." This interpretation would be correct if we were to apply the year-day principle to this time period. However, recently, some Adventist scholars have questioned the validity of applying the year-day principle to every minute time period spoken of in Revelation. For example, Revelation 17:12 says that ten horns, or nations, "for one hour will receive authority as kings along with the beast." On the year-day principle, one hour would be fifteen days.* Revelation 18:10, 17, 19 also speak of one hour, so does this mean that we should we interpret these hours as representing fifteen days, or should we understand this to mean simply a very short time? I have no burden to debate this minor detail. The point is that the time of trouble will be very short, almost certainly not more than a year, and possibly much less. Thus, when we recognize that probation has closed and the seven last plagues have begun, we can also know that Jesus' second coming is indeed "right around the corner"!

---

* This conclusion is reached by dividing the 360 days in a prophetic year by the twenty-four hours in a day, which yields fifteen days.

CHAPTER 21

The End of the Delay

The second coming of Christ will be the most dramatic event in the history of the world. Revelation says that there will be

> flashes of lightning, rumblings, peals of thunder and a severe earthquake. No earthquake like it has ever occurred since man has been on earth, so tremendous was the quake. . . . Every island fled away and the mountains could not be found. From the sky huge hailstones about a hundred pounds each fell on people (Revelation 16:18, 20, 21).

Ellen White described the second coming of Christ in similar terms and in much greater detail. She writes as one who witnessed the event:*

- Everything in nature seems turned out of its course. The streams cease to flow.
- There is a mighty earthquake. The mountains shake like reeds in the wind, and ragged rocks are scattered on every side.
- The sea is lashed into fury. There is the roar as of a coming tempest—

---

* Seventh-day Adventists believe that she actually did see the second coming of Christ in prophetic vision.

the shriek of a hurricane like the voice of demons upon a mission of destruction.

- The whole earth heaves and swells like the waves of the sea. Its surface is breaking up. Its very foundations seem to be giving way.
- Mountain chains are sinking. Inhabited islands disappear.
- The seaports that have become like Sodom for wickedness are swallowed up by the angry waters.
- The proudest cities of the earth are laid low. The lordly palaces, upon which the world's great men have lavished their wealth in order to glorify themselves, crumble to ruin before their eyes.[1]

These descriptions make it obvious that the second coming of Christ will leave the world an absolute wreck. The tall skyscrapers in the world's great cities will be rubble on the streets. Highways will have buckled and shattered, and their bridges will have collapsed. The infrastructure that has made possible life on earth as we know it today will be utterly destroyed.

However, one glorious outcome will result from this global upheaval: The graves of the redeemed from ages past will break open, and the righteous dead will be raised to life. Those who live to see Jesus come, who a short time before were being hunted down like dogs, will be changed "in the twinkling of an eye" (1 Corinthians 15:52), and all of God's people, now youthful and immortal, will be lifted from the earth "to meet the Lord in the air" (1 Thessalonians 4:17).

This will truly be the end of the delay in Christ's return!

However, it will not be the end of the delay in its fullest sense. We typically think of Christ's second coming as what's being delayed, and His return certainly will be a milestone in the plan of salvation, one that is second only to His death. However, as I pointed out in chapter 2, the delay began in heaven with Lucifer's rebellion against God. Ellen White says that "in great mercy, according to His divine character, God bore long with Lucifer."[2] How long did God wait to act? Mrs. White doesn't say. However, if "long" had the same meaning in heaven as it has on this earth, it could mean that many years passed. And as the unrest caused by

Satan's rebellion grew, the loyal angels would surely have come to Michael (Christ) and said, "Lucifer's dissatisfaction is really becoming intolerable. When are You and the Father going to do something about it?" And Michael would have responded, "I understand your concern, but the time hasn't come yet. Trust Me; when the time comes, the Father and I will act."

And, in due time, God did act. Revelation says, "There was war in heaven. Michael and his angels fought against the dragon, and the dragon and his angels fought back. But he was not strong enough, and they lost their place in heaven. The great dragon was hurled down—that ancient serpent called the devil, or Satan, who leads the whole world astray. He was hurled to the earth, and his angels with him" (12:7–9).

My point in chapter 2 was that the delay actually began in heaven prior to the creation of our world. While it's understandable that we should think of the delay in terms of Christ's second coming, in God's overall scheme of things the delay involves the entire great controversy between Christ and Satan. And that delay won't be over until the conflict between good and evil is finally resolved—at least a thousand years after Christ's second coming!

The millennium

Why will the delay not have run its course till a thousand years after Christ's second coming? I don't think we'll be able to fully understand the answer to that question until we reach heaven. However, I will make three suggestions.

Judgment. Revelation 20 contains the description of the millennium, and verse 4 of that chapter says that God's people will be "given authority to judge." As I noted in chapter 4 of my book *The Case for the Investigative Judgment,*[3] I've concluded that the judgment doesn't do anything for God. Rather, God conducts the trial, the judgment, to benefit all the intelligent beings He has created—to give all of His creatures an opportunity to examine His handling of the conflict between good and evil so they can understand why He's done what He's done.

Adventists have traditionally understood God's final judgment to involve three phases:

1. *A pre-Advent, investigative judgment* by the angels in heaven. This judgment is described in Daniel 7:9, 10, 21, 22, 26. During this judgment, heaven's books, which record the thoughts and deeds of each person who has ever claimed to serve God, will be opened for inspection. These books reveal the reasons for God's judgments, His decisions regarding the eternal fate of every human being and regarding every other aspect of the great controversy. God will respond to all questions until every angel is satisfied that Satan's charges against Him and His people are false and He is right in all of His determinations.

2. *A millennial judgment,* during which the redeemed will have an opportunity to review the history of the world and the great controversy, raise any question they wish, and see for themselves the answers in heaven's record books.

3. *A final judgment following the millennium,* when God will reveal to the wicked the reasons for His judgment against them.

Why does the millennial judgment take a thousand years? I certainly don't claim to have a good answer to that question. However, I will point out that God's redeemed will number in the billions and probably even the trillions. I'm sure heaven's record books are far superior to anything we can possibly conceive of even with our most sophisticated technology. Nevertheless, I can certainly understand the need for time to give all of those who are saved the opportunity to review heaven's record books, ask all of their questions, and get all the answers.

Cultural adaptation. Second, we may need a thousand years in heaven because we'll be experiencing a huge culture shock that will require adaptations that exceed our wildest imaginings. We'll need to learn all kinds of lessons. While I certainly don't think sin will exist in heaven, God and the angels will surely have to spend a lot of time helping us to work through some of the remaining quirks in our characters.

Training for our work in eternity. We know little about what God plans for His people throughout eternity. However, Ellen White said, "There the grandest enterprises [will] be carried forward, the loftiest aspirations reached, the highest ambitions realized."[4] What will be the nature of these grand enterprises, these lofty aspirations, these high ambitions? We have no idea. However, perhaps God will need the time during the millennium to educate us regarding these great enterprises.

I'm sure that God will keep us very busy during the millennium. And since we'll already be in heaven, the delay during those thousand years won't be painful to us the way the delay in Christ's return is today.

The end of the millennium

The delay will continue even beyond the end of the millennium because God's work of dealing with the conflict between good and evil will still not have been completed. God's grand, overall purpose is for the entire universe—every intelligent created being—to understand His great love and the justice of His way of dealing with evil. And at the end of the millennium, there will still be many humans who haven't yet gained sufficient insight.

Two great events will mark the end of the millennium: First, the descent of the heavenly city to the earth. John said that he envisioned "the Holy City, the new Jerusalem, coming down out of heaven from God" (Revelation 21:2). And second, the resurrection of the wicked of all ages (see Revelation 20:5). These people will come from their graves with the same physical, mental, and spiritual defects that they had when they died. More important, they will still share Satan's evil nature and will be loyal to his rebellion against God.

You would think that by this time Satan would be convinced that he had lost his conflict with the Trinity. But such is the deceptive nature of evil that he will make one final, desperate attempt to take over the rulership of the universe. He will rally his evil angels and the humans who have turned away from God in an attempt to storm the New Jerusalem. Revelation says that "they marched across the breadth of the earth and surrounded the camp of God's people, the city he loves" (Revelation 20:9).

Ellen White's description is much more detailed. She says that Satan will consult with his angels and then with the kings and military leaders who have been raised from the dead. They will look upon the strength and numbers on their side and declare that the army within the city is small in comparison with theirs, and that it can be overcome. They lay their plans to take possession of the riches and glory of the New Jerusalem. All immediately begin to prepare for battle. Skillful artisans construct implements of war. Military leaders, famed for their success, marshal the throngs of warlike men into companies and divisions.[5]

Please consider for a moment the implication of Ellen White's description. Satan will strategize with his angels and the people who have cast their lot with him on how to take the New Jerusalem. Skillful artisans will have to construct implements of war. Military leaders will have to train their captains, their lieutenants, and their foot soldiers on how to fight. *All of this will take time.*

Then consider this: The second coming of Christ will have left the world an absolute wreck; thus, the hosts of evil will also have to embark on a huge reconstruction program. Buildings will have to be erected; highways will have to be rebuilt; and communication systems will have to be restored. Satan's human followers will also have to eat in order to survive, so some of his forces will have to devote themselves to farming the land and growing the food. It took years for humans to build the infrastructure we enjoy today, and it isn't likely that Satan and his evil hosts can accomplish it overnight, even with their supernatural powers. We don't know how long the process of restoring the infrastructure and creating war machines will take, but it will very likely take years, *and this will all be part of that overarching delay.*

Finally, the preparations for war will be completed, and Satan and his officers will give the order to advance.

The countless host moves on—an army such as was never summoned by earthly conquerors, such as the combined forces of all ages since war began on earth could never equal. Satan, the mightiest of warriors, leads the van, and his angels unite their forces for this final struggle. . . . With military precision the serried ranks advance over the earth's broken and uneven surface to the city of God. By command of Jesus, the gates of the New Jerusalem are closed, and the armies of Satan surround the city and make ready for the onset.[6]

However, before the wicked can attack, a throne will begin to rise above the Holy City. John says, "I saw a great white throne and him who was seated on it. Earth and sky fled from his presence, and there was no place for them. And I saw the dead, great and small, standing before the throne" (Revelation 20:11, 12). Ellen White said that "upon this throne sits the Son of God. . . . The power and majesty of Christ no language can describe, no pen portray."[7]

Then heaven's record books will once more be opened. We must not think of these books as dusty tomes sitting on a shelf. God's method of keeping records is surely vastly superior to what we can do with even our most sophisticated computers. Indeed, God's records can probably be played back in something like our 3-D or holographic formats. God will portray before the assembled hosts of the universe—both the righteous and the wicked—the great scenes in the history of the great controversy: Satan's rebellion in heaven, the temptation and fall of Adam and Eve, and especially the life and death of Jesus. "Before the swaying multitude are revealed the final scenes [of Christ's life]—the patient Sufferer treading the path to Calvary; the prince of heaven hanging upon the cross. . . . The awful spectacle appears just as it was."[8]

Satan will stand paralyzed. He will think back to his rebellion against Christ in heaven. He will recall the moral evil and the horrible suffering he has brought on the human race during the six thousand years of its existence. And he will see that "his voluntary rebellion has unfitted him for heaven. . . . Satan bows down and confesses the justice of his sentence."[9] Then the entire multitude of evil human beings and angels bow before Christ and acknowledge His supremacy, thus fulfilling Paul's statement that "at the name of Jesus every knee [will] bow, in heaven and on earth and under the earth, and every tongue confess that Jesus Christ is Lord, to the glory of God the Father" (Philippians 2:10, 11).

In a formal debate and in a court of law, the best evidence in support of a particular conclusion is the agreement of the opposition that their opponents' case is correct, and that is precisely what Satan and all of his hosts will provide at the close of the millennium. Those who have been declared guilty in the final judgment will agree that God is right, that their sentence is just. *This is the resolution to the great controversy that God has been moving toward from the moment that Satan first rebelled against Him in heaven.*

However, in spite of his acknowledgement that God is right, Satan will not surrender.

> The spirit of rebellion, like a mighty torrent, again bursts forth. Filled with frenzy, he [Satan] determines not to yield the great controversy. The time has come for a last desperate struggle against the King of heaven. He rushes into the midst of his subjects and endeavors to inspire them with his own fury and arouse them to instant battle. But of all the countless millions whom he has allured into rebellion, there are none now to acknowledge his supremacy. His power is at an end. The wicked are filled with the same hatred of God that inspires Satan; but they see that their case is hopeless, that they cannot prevail against Jehovah. Their rage is kindled against Satan and those who have been his agents in deception, and with the fury of demons they turn on them.[10]

Then fire will descend from heaven and consume them. The Bible calls this the "lake of fire." John said, "Death and Hades were thrown into the lake of fire. The lake of fire is the second death. Anyone whose name was not found written in the book of life was thrown into the lake of fire" (Revelation 20:14, 15).

Now the memorable words of the last paragraph of Ellen White's book *The Great Controversy* will be fulfilled.

> The great controversy is ended. Sin and sinners are no more. The entire universe is clean. One pulse of harmony and gladness

beats through the vast creation. From Him who created all, flow life and light and gladness, throughout the realms of illimitable space. From the minutest atom to the greatest world, all things, animate and inanimate, in their unshadowed beauty and perfect joy, declare that God is love.[11]

The delay is finally over!

---

1. White, *The Great Controversy,* 636, 637.

2. White, *Patriarchs and Prophets,* 39.

3. Marvin Moore, *The Case for the Investigative Judgment* (Nampa, ID: Pacific Press®, 2010), 37–46.

4. White, *The Great Controversy,* 677.

5. Ibid., 664.

6. Ibid.

7. Ibid., 665.

8. Ibid., 667.

9. Ibid., 670.

10. Ibid., 671, 672.

11. Ibid., 678.

ADDENDUM:

Two Views of the Millennium

Most Christians today believe that Christ will reign on the earth following His second coming. They also believe that both the righteous and the wicked will dwell together, the difference being that whereas before Christ's second coming the forces of evil dominated the world's political systems, after the Second Coming, Christ and His followers will be in control.

Seventh-day Adventists disagree with this conclusion for at least three reasons. First, there is not the slightest hint in Scripture that the righteous and the wicked will live together following the Second Coming. To the contrary, Jesus said, "When the Son of Man comes in his glory, and all the angels with him, . . . he will separate the people from one another as a shepherd separates the sheep from the goats" (Matthew 25:31, 32). And in the parable of the wheat and the weeds, Jesus said that at the end of the age

> the Son of Man will send out his angels, and they will weed out of his kingdom everything that causes sin and all who do evil. They will throw them into the blazing furnace, where there will be weeping and gnashing of teeth. Then the righteous will shine like the sun in the kingdom of their Father (Matthew 13:41–43).

Second, according to both the Bible and Ellen White, following Christ's second coming, the world will be a shattered wreck. It is unimaginable that Christ would require His people to dwell in the midst of that devastation, where they would have to spend years upon years to make the world habitable again.

Third, Jesus assured His disciples—and us—that He was going to His Father's house "to prepare a place for you. And if I go and prepare a place for you, I will come back and take you to be with me *that you also may be where I am*" (John 14:2, 3; emphasis added). When Jesus comes back, He will take us to be with Him so that where He is *now*, we will be *then*—in heaven, not on a shattered planet living side by side with the wicked.

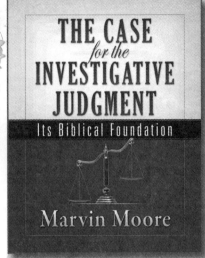